THE WAR

IN PICTURES

SIXTH YEAR

———

ODHAMS PRESS LIMITED

LONG ACRE. LONDON. W. C. 2

VICTORY SCENE IN LONDON
owds gathered in front of Buckingham
Palace on VJ-Day, 15 August, 1945.

YEAR OF VICTORY

THE first days of the sixth and final year of the Second World War saw the powerful Allied armies in the West racing across France and Belgium towards the frontier of Germany along the Rhine. Very considerable progress had been made in the three eventful months since D-Day, when the Anglo-American forces made their initial landing on the northwest coast of Nazi-occupied Europe. Once the hard core of the enemy's resistance had been broken and a break-through achieved by the decisive victory around Caen, the Allied drive eastwards from the Normandy bridgehead gained rapid momentum. Paris was freed on 25 August, and little more than a week later, on 3 September, the British Second Army liberated the heroic Belgian capital which had suffered under the cruel German occupation for more than four years.

Although there was still a good deal of hard and bitter fighting to come, through a winter which brought extreme weather conditions, it was now clearly evident that the fate of Nazi Germany was sealed. Nor could the promised invasion of Hitler's " impregnable " Reich be much longer delayed, in spite of all the cunning tactics and surprises that the enemy might use. Not only had the German war leaders to face imminent invasion by six brilliantly led and well-equipped armies advancing from the west of the Rhine, but mighty new blows were being prepared by the Red Army in the east, particularly against East Prussia, the traditional home of German militarism.

Meanwhile, the German people themselves, whose morale had been greatly weakened by a long series of military defeats and greater privations at home, were suffering the most tremendous air assault of the war, carried on by the powerful Allied air forces operating from bases not only in Britain but on the Continent as well. The heavy and continuous bombing of centres of war production, communications and garrison and fortified towns throughout the Reich played a foremost part in the glorious victory of Allied arms and saved many thousands of British and

3

ALLIED SEA POWER IN THE PACIFIC. Throughout the final year of the war the Allied navies had absolute command of the world's seas. In a great sea battle off the Philippine Islands towards the end of October, 1944, the Japanese fleet was decisively beaten. Powerful American battleships, such as the one shown here in action off the coasts of Okinawa, played an important part in the conquest of island bases on the way to Japan itself.

American lives. The Allies now held undisputed mastery in the skies over Germany itself.

After the rapid advance made by the Western Allies across France and Belgium into Holland, it seemed likely at first that they might well succeed in gaining a bridgehead over the Rhine delta before the enemy found time to recover and make a fresh stand. To this end one of the most audacious military operations of the war was planned and executed by the Allied High Command. On 17 September thousands of paratroops and glider-borne infantry were dropped around Arnhem and Nijmegen in Holland to seize the crossings of the rivers Waal and Lek, two main branches of the Rhine, while British armour thrust forward over the Mass-Scheldt Canal to link up with them.

This operation, in which the 1st British Paratroop Division showed outstanding valour in their stand at Arnhem, was undertaken at considerable risk in the knowledge that its success would probably shorten the war in Europe by several months. It nearly did succeed. The bridges over

the river at Nijmegen were captured but it was not possible to hold out against overwhelming numbers of the enemy at Arnhem, where bad weather conditions prevented sufficient reinforcements of supplies by air. By 25-26 September, when it was realized that the bid had failed, the gallant survivors of the airborne forces were withdrawn from Arnhem. Only about one-third of the 8,000 men dropped came back.

Meanwhile, very notable progress had been made by the American Seventh Army fighting on the most southerly sector of the Western Front. Driving northwards from the Mediterranean coast through the Rhone valley, with the aid of the rising French patriot forces, they liberated the great city of Lyons and pressed on towards the Belfort Gap and the Rhine beyond Mulhouse, meeting comparatively light resistance from the disorganized enemy troops in the district. Farther to the north considerable advances eastwards to the highly industrialized Saar Basin were made by General Patton's Third Army. The American First and Ninth Armies made progress against stiffer German opposition north and south of the ancient German city of Aachen, captured when it had been virtually reduced to a heap of ruins. Right along the Western Front the great autumn offensive of the Allied armies pressing to the Rhine was going well.

With the German Luftwaffe practically driven from the skies everywhere, the autumn of 1944 saw the second of Hitler's retaliatory " secret weapons " put into operation. Soon after the Allies had made their first landings in Normandy early in the summer, the enemy launched pilotless aircraft, or flying bombs, against Southern England from bases situated chiefly in the French coastal area of the Pas de Calais. These were now supplanted by a more deadly long-range rocket weapon, launched from the north of Holland. While this new weapon was appreciably less accurate in finding targets than the flying bomb, no warning could be given of its approach and, moreover, there was no effective means of defence against it. The rockets caused a great deal of damage and much loss of life among civilians, particularly in the London area, but its effect on the great Allied offensives in Western Europe was,

in fact, negligible. It was now too late for the Nazis to try and alter the course of the war by such methods.

By the middle of December, however, the German commander on the Western Front, von Rundstedt, decided to stake almost everything that he had in men and materials on an all-out counter-offensive to drive the Allies back from the vital approaches to the Rhine, the last great barrier before the heart of Germany. It was the Nazis' final throw on land. In preparation for this the enemy had contrived to build up quite a substantial reserve and had, in fact, two new types of tank to put into the field. Even the depleted German air force was temporarily resuscitated with fast jet-propelled aircraft, which proved quite effective in the first stages of the attack.

At dawn on 16 December a full-scale armour attack, the biggest since the fighting in Normandy, was flung against the weakest part of the line held by General Hodges's First Army, between Monschau and Trier in the Belgian Ardennes. The attack was violent and of such strength that within only two or three days a gap of some twenty-five miles had been torn in the American-

MASSACRE IN A FRENCH TOWN. One of the vilest Nazi crimes against civilians took place in the French town of Oradour-sur-Glane. After shooting all the male inhabitants, German troops herded the women and children into the church which was then locked and set ablaze with petrol. Afterwards the rest of the town was fired. The shell of Oradour-sur-Glane church is shown above with the altar tablet commemorating the victims.

LANDING SUPPLIES ON OKINAWA
The conquest of this vital island base, less than 400 miles from the Japanese homeland, by the Americans was one of the most bitterly fought campaigns of the Pacific war.

HARD FIGHTING IN ITALY. Although the last stages of the difficult campaign in Italy were rather over-shadowed by events taking place on other fronts in Europe, the Fifth and Eighth Armies made good progress in driving the Germans steadily from the Apennine Mountains into the plains of North Italy. In this picture men of the Eighth Army are seen entering the war-scarred town of Portomaggiore on their way towards Bologna

held positions, and the enemy had thrown no fewer than fourteen or fifteen divisions into his offensive. Von Rundstedt's well-organized plan was to disrupt the Allied communications so thoroughly as to prevent any renewed push towards the Rhine for some considerable time. It also became clear that his primary objective was the very important communications centre of Liége, the capture of which might have had the most serious and far-reaching consequences for the Allies.

After nearly ten days of hard and confused fighting in the Ardennes salient, during which time the bad weather conditions had favoured the enemy, the Germans had penetrated more than fifty miles into Belgium and were within four of the Meuse. Then General Eisenhower placed the American forces north of the break-through under command of Field-Marshal Montgomery and, fighting together as one team, they at last halted Rundstedt's offensive. The great speed with which the Allies consolidated their northern flank finally removed the threat to Liége. By the end of December the worst of the Ardennes crisis was

over. In the middle of January, after the Germans had begun a major withdrawal from the salient, big new attacks by the British in the north and by General Patton's Third Army in the south flung the enemy back to his original positions. Rundstedt's last throw had failed and the Germans were poorer by no fewer than 90,000 men which they could ill afford to spare.

On the Eastern Front, meanwhile, the Red Army had launched powerful and decisive blows against the Germans in the Balkans, in Poland, and in the Baltic States in preparation for the final Russian drive into East Prussia, Austria and Germany itself. On 23 October Red Army divisions under Marshal Chernyakhovsky invaded German East Prussia on a front of eighty-five miles. Here, however, the enemy put in some fierce counter-attacks, and after making a swift initial advance the Red Army's victorious progress was temporarily brought to a standstill in a heavily fortified zone. Nevertheless, the fact that the Russians had gained a solid footing within the borders of the Reich had its effect upon the deteriorating morale both of the German armed forces and the civilian population. Mass exits of civilians from East Prussia, fleeing in the face of the Red Army, further harassed the already overstrained rail and road communications of Eastern Germany.

Far to the south, in the Balkans, Marshal Tolbukhin's forces had entered Transylvania and from there advanced up both banks of the Danube towards Budapest, while another army was fighting its way down through the Carpathian passes to the north. By December the capital city of Hungary was surrounded by the Russians and all efforts by the Germans to break out failed. After many weeks of some of the most desperate street and house-to-house battles since the siege of Stalingrad, the German garrison at Budapest was wiped out and the city occupied by the Russians on 13 February. Meanwhile, the Germans had been liquidated in Yugoslavia, while in Poland vast Russian forces under Marshals Koniev and Zhukov smashed across the plains and liberated the stricken capital city of Warsaw and the important centre of Cracow, heading for the line of the Oder, the last river barrier before Berlin. In East Prussia, too, the offensive had been renewed by the Red Army and the German

defenders were being driven back against the Baltic coast or into isolated pockets around Danzig, Koenigsberg and elsewhere. Their position was rapidly becoming hopeless.

In Italy the Fifth and Eighth Armies smashed through the German " Gothic Line " north of Florence in the early weeks of the autumn. Much steady progress was made in the direction of Bologna, the Eighth Army capturing the great town of Ravenna, but the going was particularly difficult through the mountainous terrain. Although the Allied advance in Italy was therefore much less spectacular than on other fronts in Europe, the armies fighting there were doing good work by pinning down large enemy forces which the German High Command needed so badly to replace their losses elsewhere. Throughout the autumn and winter months, too, American heavy bombers operating from Italian bases carried on the vital task of wrecking industrial plants in the Reich and disorganizing the enemy's communications, especially through the Brenner Pass leading into Austria.

Meanwhile, in the Far East, large-scale Allied operations were carrying the war ever nearer to the Japanese homeland with the acquisition of

ADVANCE IN BURMA. In the early months of 1945 great advances were made by British and Indian troops of the Fourteenth Army in Burma. The fall of Mandalay on 20 March, after a hard battle against the enemy defences in Fort Dufferin, marked the climax of the arduous three-year campaign. Some six weeks later the Fourteenth Army were in Rangoon. Above, troops charge into the burning town of Meiktila, eighty miles south of Mandalay.

valuable bases in the Central Pacific. The most important of these operations was the reconquest of the Philippine Islands, where powerful landings were made along the west coast of Leyte in October. Successes against the Japanese on Leyte were followed in the next few months by landings on the other main Philippine Islands of Mindoro, Luzon and Mindanao, the capture of which gave the Allies a central key-point for all future operations and threatened to cut the enemy's communications with all his outlying conquests. In a great naval battle fought off the Philippines towards the end of October, the Japanese Fleet was severely crippled with the loss of two large battleships, four carriers and eight cruisers, besides a number of smaller ships. British and American submarines continued to take heavy toll of enemy shipping in Far Eastern waters.

In Europe the Western Front flared into activity again in the last week of February, when Field-Marshal Montgomery launched a smashing offensive against the German forces west of the Rhine. These great battles, in which British, American and Canadian forces all took part, were to be decisive in bringing about the final collapse of Hitler's armies in the West. From Nijmegen south to Venlo a tremendous weight of Allied armour was thrown against the enemy, and the Allies were swift in following up their initial successes. The Americans forced a crossing of the Roer River and captured Julich and Duren and came close to the huge Rhineland city of Cologne. British and Canadian troops fought grim battles against the frantic enemy, especially around the strong-points of Goch and Cleve, to reach the Rhine at Wesel. Some of the toughest fighting west of the river took place in the region of Xanten, near the Wesel crossing, where British infantry waged a bloody but victorious battle against numbers of fanatical German paratroops.

Hard as the enemy fought back from key strong-points which guarded the Rhine, the fury of the Allied onslaught could not be halted. Farther to the south troops of General Patton's Third Army were advancing through the defences of the

BRITISH TROOPS CROSS THE RHINE. The crossing of the Rhine by armies under the command of Field-Marshal Montgomery on 23-24 March, 1945, was, after D-Day, one of the greatest offensive operations of the war against Germany. Troops from many parts of the British Isles took part in the first crossings made opposite the fortified town of Wesel, and the picture was taken when men of the Dorset Regiment were crossing the Rhine.

LANDING ON THE OTHER SIDE. Many thousands of troops made the crossing of the Rhine in special amphibious craft known as "Buffaloes." A group of British soldiers of the Cheshire Regiment are seen here just after they had landed on the far side of the river. These men were some of the first to cross the Rhine to support the force of British Commandos, the advance guard detailed to capture Wesel in the opening phase of the offensive.

Siegfried Line, beating the Germans back relentlessly. By the end of the first week in March the Allies had reached the Rhine along a continuous stretch of about 150 miles from Nijmegen almost to Coblenz. Cologne, third largest city of Germany, fell on 6 March and two days later the Americans achieved the first crossing of the Rhine at Remagen. The enemy had planned to blow up the bridge here, but American patrols disconnected the fuses attached to the mines just in time, and soon tanks and infantry were pouring across in great strength despite artillery fire from defenders on the opposite bank.

The main crossings of the Rhine by the 21st Army Group under command of Field-Marshal Montgomery took place on the night of 23-24 March. The river was forced on a twenty-five-mile front to the north of the Ruhr, and among the first troops to get across were men of the 15th and 51st Scottish Divisions. This operation, magnificently planned and brilliantly executed in the true Montgomery tradition, was on such a vast scale that it was something like another D-Day. It was carried out under cover of the biggest smoke screen in the history of warfare and this helped considerably to mislead the enemy.

Air support was given on a tremendous scale and this, together with the mighty artillery barrage directed across the river, made life for the defenders on the approaches to the east bank of the Rhine almost impossible. British Commando troops had been sent across the river at ten o'clock in the evening on 23 March, before the main crossings began, to capture the key town of Wesel, probably the most strongly defended German position of all across the Lower Rhine. Then about an hour later the air attack opened against Wesel, and the town was pulverized to a heap of rubble with only the shells of a few buildings left standing. The same fate overtook every strong-point which the enemy had built up in the line of the Allied advance, making his position everywhere a hopeless one.

The battle for the Rhine crossings was a combined operation in every sense. Even British and U.S. naval forces were brought in to provide special ferry craft for the troops and trained crews to man them. Meanwhile, more than 10,000 engineers were engaged in assembling pontoons and making bridges; they worked with such speed that within a few hours after the first troops had got across the Rhine the first complete

ESSEN CAPTURED. On 10 April, 1945, the American Ninth Army occupied the great German industrial city of Essen. This was the home of the Krupp armament works and centre of the Ruhr coal-mining and steel industry, with a normal population of about 660,000. The Krupp works, the ruins of which are shown here, received the

attention of the R.A.F. quite early in the war. From 1943 onwards this huge armaments centre was bombed with increasing force by day and night, and by December, 1944, the Krupp output had been reduced to less than one third of its normal. On 11 March, 1945, the heaviest attack by over 1,000 bombers finally destroyed it.

13

bridge was carrying over reinforcements and supplies. On 24 March the greatest airborne landing of the war was made east of the river by the First Allied Airborne Army, and these sky troops distinguished themselves in capturing many vital key points and rounding up thousands of prisoners. The lessons of Arnhem had been well learnt for this airborne operation was a complete success, everything going to a clockwork plan.

WEHRMACHT BREAKS UP

Now the Western Allies had forced the last and most formidable obstacle barring the way to the heart of the Reich. The enemy's last line of defence was shattered and the Wehrmacht was about to break up rapidly before the immense pressure of men and arms ranged against them. Ahead of the advancing tank columns, which were fanning out in all directions across Germany, went the British and American bombers, destroying the enemy's communications and breaking up his last-ditch defences everywhere. In those memorable weeks of April, when famous German towns and cities were surrendering to the Allies one after another, demoralized enemy soldiers were being rounded up by hundreds of thousands. In many places the hordes of men coming out to give themselves up on the roads delayed the great advance. Only in such key cities as Leipzig, Nuremberg and Bremen was any resistance found, but even this was quickly smashed.

In the East, meanwhile, the Russians had won a decisive victory by forcing a crossing of the Oder. This opened up the way to Berlin itself and made it quite impossible for the enemy to delay the final crushing onslaught by the Red Army. Marshal Koniev's men had captured the big city of Breslau, for which the Germans had fought bitterly, and occupied the great industrial area of Upper Silesia. Farther to the south other powerful Russian forces were driving on to Vienna, captured by Marshal Tolbukhin on 13 April, and outflanking most of Austria. In Czechoslovakia, the Red Army was heading towards Prague, last of the capital cities of Europe to be freed from the hated Nazi yoke. Both in Austria and Czechoslovakia the Russians were helped in their great task by local bands of anti-fascists who had risen in great numbers against their oppressors. Although the German High Command transferred masses of men and material from the West to try and stem the forward surge of the Red Army, they were now hopelessly outmanœuvred. The hour of Germany's total defeat was imminent.

As the Allies advanced deeper into the heart of the Reich, the most appalling horrors of Nazi rule came to light in the notorious concentration camps at Dachau, Belsen, Buchenwald, Nordhausen and elsewhere. In all these camps mass torture and cruelty had been practised for years on a scale that almost defied the imagination. Tens of thousands of victims—men, women and little children—were found dead and dying amid indescribable conditions. Here, revealed to a profoundly shocked world, was staggering evidence of the Nazis' policy of mass extermination of Jews, democrats, communists and antifascists from all over Europe. Many of the wretched victims who had been starved, beaten or otherwise tortured to death were entirely innocent of any crime.

By the beginning of May the complete collapse of Nazi Germany was an accomplished fact. The long, hard-fought campaign in Italy was brought to an end with the unconditional surrender of nearly one million German troops to Field-Marshal Alexander on 29 April. On the previous day Mussolini, first of the Fascist dictators, had been shot dead by Italian partisans while trying to escape justice. On 2 May, after three weeks of unabated street fighting, the Berlin garrison capitulated and the Red Army had achieved its greatest triumph of the war. More than 100,000 Germans were killed during the battle for Berlin, and both Hitler and Goebbels were reported to have died in the doomed city. Many other Nazi leaders and war criminals who were still at large had taken an insecure refuge in the mountains of Bavaria and Austria, where they were soon to be rounded up by swiftly advancing Allied columns which were closing in from the north-west.

UNCONDITIONAL SURRENDER

On 4 May German emissaries went to Field-Marshal Montgomery's headquarters near Hamburg to agree to the unconditional terms for their armies in North-West Germany, Holland and Denmark. At Rheims, on 7 May, General Bedell Smith, Chief of Staff to General Eisenhower, received Germany's unconditional surrender and the terms were duly signed. Then in Berlin, on 9 May, the same terms were signed in the presence of the Russians, the Prussian Field-Marshal Keitel, Chief of the German Army High Command, putting his signature to the document of surrender.

The end of the war in Europe was celebrated with rejoicing by peoples all over the world; in the former Nazi-occupied countries of Europe people wept with heartfelt relief and joy when they realized the nightmare of the past five and a half years was at last finished and done with. Troops of the Allied nations who had played a part in the glorious liberation of a continent received a tremendous welcome wherever they appeared. Meanwhile, in London, hundreds of thousands

conditions in the world, was brought to a triumphant end at the beginning of May when the Fourteenth Army entered Rangoon. Those troops who had waged jungle and mountain warfare against the Japanese in Burma for three and a half years had received little of the limelight focused on events elsewhere, but their brave achievements will long live in the annals of military history.

TRUMAN WITH ROOSEVELT. The death of President Roosevelt on 12 April, 1945, robbed the United Nations of one of their greatest leaders, and America of an inspiring national figure. Franklin D. Roosevelt was succeeded by Vice-President Truman, and in one of the last photographs taken of President Roosevelt they are seen together.

of people stood in the streets around Whitehall to give an ovation to Mr. Winston Churchill, the hero of the hour, whose daring leadership had brought Britain safely through the darkest days in her history.

While the war in Europe was over, the final struggle against the treacherous enemy in the Far East had still to be won. Yet, in those early days of May, few could have believed that Japan would be brought to her knees in less than four months after the defeat of Germany. Factors yet unknown, however, were to shorten the final battles.

The long campaign in Burma, fought largely by British troops across more than a thousand miles of the most difficult country and worst climatic

They played a great part in the Far East war as a whole, inflicting well over a quarter of a million casualties on the enemy and pinning down large forces he could have used elsewhere.

From early April until 21 June the Americans fought one of the most bitter campaigns of the whole war on the Pacific island of Okinawa. The Japanese put up the most determined resistance to try and prevent this vital strip of land from becoming an Allied base for bombing raids against their homeland. In doing so they lost over 100,000 dead. Meanwhile, the large group of Philippine Islands were finally cleared of the enemy. Farther to the south the Australians were engaged in the task of driving the Japanese from

THANKSGIVING FOR VICTORY
Their Majesties the King and Queen, with Princess Elizabeth and Princess Margaret, arrive at St. Paul's Cathedral in London for the National Thanksgiving Service.

Borneo. Two weeks after the Australian 9th Division had made their successful landings on the coast of British North Borneo on 10 June, they had cleared the important Seria oilfields. In July further landings were made near Balikpapan, in South-East Borneo, where strong enemy resistance had to be overcome.

Meanwhile, increasingly heavy raids were being made on the big cities of Japan by fleets of American " Super-Fortresses " flying from newly won bases in the Pacific and from China. Many attacks were also launched from aircraft carriers which steamed in company with the British and American fleets in Japanese home waters. On 10 July about 2,000 carrier-based aircraft attacked scores of important targets in and around Tokyo, and although the American carrier force was only within fifteen minutes' flying time of Tokyo Bay, not a single Japanese warship or aircraft gave battle.

On 6 August the first atomic bomb ever to be used in war was dropped on the Japanese city and naval base of Hiroshima. A second atomic bomb fell on Nagasaki three days later. These bombs, the most powerful weapon ever devised by man, obliterated everything over a very wide area and killed every living thing which lay in the way. About a third of the total population of each city was wiped out. On 8 August the Soviet Union declared war on Japan, and within a few days the Russian armies had advanced deeply into Manchuria where much of the remaining military strength was concentrated.

These events brought about the swift collapse of the Japanese Empire and by the middle of August the last of the enemies had decided to accept the Allied terms for unconditional surrender as declared by the leaders of Britain, America and China at the Potsdam conference a few weeks previously. The Japanese Emperor himself broadcast surrender orders to his troops who were still fighting on many scattered fronts. The first surrender talks were opened at Manila, capital of the Philippine Islands, early in the morning of 19 August. On 26 August Japanese envoys were flown to Rangoon to accept terms for the surrender of Burma and Malaya. Four days later General MacArthur, Commander-in-Chief of the Allied forces, arrived on the mainland of Japan itself, and on 2 September, the final surrender terms were signed aboard the American battleship, *Missouri*, anchored in Tokyo Bay. Peace had at last come to the whole world after exactly six years of the greatest and most terrible war in history.

LIBERATION OF BRUSSELS

3 SEPTEMBER, 1944

After a spectacular advance of seventy-three miles since sunrise, the British Second Army entered the capital city of Belgium on the evening of 3 September. First troops to reach Brussels were the Guards Armoured Division under Major-General Adair, who were closely followed by the 11th British Armoured Division commanded by General Horrocks. And so another European capital was set free after suffering the grim tyranny of German rule for more than four years. (Brussels was captured by the enemy in May, 1940, following a series of terrific air attacks by the Luftwaffe.) As the British columns entered the city again, flames were seen to be coming from the historic Palais de Justice, which the retreating enemy set on fire as a final act of vandalism. This building, most of which was destroyed, had been used as a wireless station for Nazi propaganda. In spite of the terrible ordeals which they had borne under German occupation, the people of Brussels turned out in their thousands to give their liberators a tumultuous welcome. Every street and square through which the British vehicles passed was packed with wildly cheering crowds. The swift advance of the British Second Army had taken the Germans by surprise, and while most of the enemy had made a hasty retreat a few groups of resisters were left behind. Within a short time, however, the accurate fire of guns mounted on the British tanks had eliminated the last snipers' nest. The picture on these pages shows a British armoured vehicle passing between the lines of cheering citizens in a street of Brussels.

19

REVENGE AND JOY IN BRUSSELS. Immediately after their liberation the citizens of Brussels gave vent to their angry feelings against the hated Germans. An effigy and portraits of Hitler were burnt on the steps of the town hall, while the Gestapo building was raided by patriots and all files and documents destroyed. Pictures show: above, crowds gathered outside the former headquarters of the Belgian quislings; top right, a German-owned shop in Brussels being demolished by civilians; bottom right, more cheers for British soldiers in the city.

ANTWERP CAPTURED. On 4 September the British Second Army continued its swift advance through Belgium and reached the great port of Antwerp, second largest city of the country. Here, as in Brussels, the Germans were caught completely by surprise and more than 2,000 prisoners were taken. Among them was General Graf von Stolberg, the German Commander of Antwerp, who was captured by four British privates while he

was lunching in his private house. A great round-up of trapped enemy units was made by the Belgian Forces of the Interior. Many of the captured local traitors were placed in the empty cages of the city's zoological gardens. Other important places liberated the same day were Louvain, famous in the First World War, and the industrial city of Malines. The picture reproduced on these pages shows German prisoners marching in Antwerp.

ATTACK ON THE GOTHIC LINE

In the early days of September, 1944, the German Gothic Line in the Northern Apennines of Italy was breached on a twenty-mile front in a series of very powerful attacks launched against it by the Eighth Army. Penetrations were made through the enemy's defensive positions to a depth of four miles. While these advances were being made in the Adriatic sector of the front, other troops of the Eighth Army made important progress towards the Gothic Line from positions north of Florence. All the ground troops were ably supported by the Desert Air Force, which concentrated many bomb-loads on enemy troop concentrations and supply lines. By 4 September the British and Canadians had reached a point only six miles from Rimini, the strong German-held bastion guarding the eastern approaches to the Po valley and the Plain of Lombardy. Meanwhile, the Fifth Army had launched new attacks and, with infantry and tanks, crossed the river Arno at many places between Florence and the sea. On 6 September the Americans completed the occupation of Lucca, an ancient town associated with Julius Caesar and having many historic buildings. By the capture of Monte Albano, between the Arno and Pistoia, the Fifth Army also reached the Gothic Line. In the picture a Long Tom gun crosses a Bailey bridge over the River Sieve at Borgo San Lorenzo.

TRANSPORT PROBLEMS IN ITALY. Fighting in the mountainous country of the Apennines, where many stone-built villages favoured the defenders, proved a severe test on the Allied supply and transport organization. In many places the terrain was so difficult that laden mules were used to carry supplies for the infantry. Many remarkable feats of bridge-building were achieved by Allied engineers, upon whose work the speed of the advance largely depended. Picture on left shows a Bailey bridge thrown across a 530-ft. gap on the Fifth Army front. Above, columns of transport vehicles wind over the hills after Eighth Army's great break-through.

WAR CRIMINALS ON TRIAL. During September the first trials of Nazi and Fascist war criminals were held. The picture shows a noisy scene before the trial of Caruso, ex-chief of police in Rome when angry demonstrators seized the Fascist governor of the city prison and beat him up in court. Pictures on the right were taken at the famous Lublin trial, when Nazi excutioners from the Majdanek concentration camp in Poland (where over 1,000,000 helpless civilians were murdered) were found guilty. Top, Nazi murderers on the prisoners' bench in court; below, excited crowds of Lublin civilians gathered outside the court waiting for the verdict to be announced.

QUEBEC CONFERENCE

On 10 September Mr. Churchill arrived in Canada for a week of conferences with President Roosevelt and the Combined Chiefs of Staff. Mr. Mackenzie King Premier of Canada, took part in the discussions. An invitation had been sent to Marshal Stalin who, however, was unable to leave the Soviet Union at that time. After the final meetings on 16-17 September a joint statement was issued declaring that "The President and the British Prime Minister with Combined Chiefs of Staff discussed all aspects of the war against Germany and Japan." Mr. Churchill returned in the liner "Queen Mary," reaching England on 26 September. On the right, Mr. Churchill, followed by his wife and Mr. Mackenzie King, is seen leaving train at Quebec; below, President Roosevelt and Mr. Churchill on the terrace of Quebec Citadel. Opposite page: top, Conference in session. Among figures round the table are Mr. Mackenzie King, Mr. Malcolm Macdonald (British Minister to Canada), Mr. Churchill, Field-Marshal Sir Alan Brooke, Field-Marshal Sir John Dill, Admiral Sir Andrew Cunningham and Marshal of the Royal Air Force Sir Charles Portal; below, Mr. Churchill and Mr. Mackenzie King leave the Quebec Legislature in an open car.

ATTACK ON LE HAVRE. On 12 September all enemy resistance ceased in Le Havre and the British took complete control of the port. This large French seaport had been by-passed as the Allies advanced across Northern France and Belgium, and the powerful German garrison there was under seige for several weeks. The carefully prepared assault on the town followed days and night of heavy bombardment from the air, during

which the R.A.F. dropped about 10,000 tons of bombs. Preliminary attacks were also made from the sea by the British battleship H.M.S. "Warspite" and the monitor "Erebus." The land assault on Le Havre was completed within thirty-six hours, during which the British had to break through immensely strong fortifications and many minefields. Top, flame-throwers in action in the first stages of the attack; below, tanks and infantry advancing.

Important land base

CHINESE TROOPS CAPTURE TENGCHUNG. On 14 September the Chinese High Command announced that their troops advancing from Yunnan into North Burma had taken the important city of Tengchung. This was the first big Chinese city to be recaptured after eight years of war, and as a strong Japanese base it had been the main obstacle to linking together the Burma and Ledo roads. The battle lasted five weeks and 3,000 Japanese died in the fighting. Top left and right, Chinese in Tengchung again; above, Chinese gunners in hills above Tengchung.

AMERICANS ATTACK PALAU ISLANDS. On 14 September U.S. Marines and Army assault groups landed on Peleliu Island in the Palau group, Western Carolines. The Palau group of islands was the last stronghold of the Japanese in the Central Pacific and the key area to the Philippines, only 450 miles away. After twelve days of bitter fighting, during which the Japanese lost about 10,000 in killed alone, Peleliu was in American hands except for isolated pockets of resistance in the north and south. On 16 September successful landings were also made on Anguar, the southernmost island of the group. On the left, U.S. landing craft are seen heading for Anguar Island; above, busy scene on a beach at Peleliu as ammunition and supplies are taken ashore for the invading forces.

AIRBORNE ARMY INVADES HOLLAND

17 SEPTEMBER, 1944

A broadcast message from SHAEF on 17 September announced that strong forces of the First Allied Airborne Army had just landed in Holland. In this, the greatest single airborne operation yet launched, well over 1,000 tow planes and gliders took part. Among the thousands of paratroops and glider-borne infantry were British, American and Polish units with Dutch Commando detachments. The whole operation was commanded by Lieutenant-General Lewis H. Brereton. Equipment included light guns and jeeps, as well as large quantities of ammunition, food and smaller weapons. Landings were made in the Rhine delta of Holland, on the right flank of the German defence line in the West and ahead of the British Second Army. The great task of the airborne forces was to hold the vital Arnhem bridges until the British Second Army had advanced through Holland to join up with them, thereby turning the line of the Rhine and opening the way into the heart of Germany. It was a brilliant plan, and the airborne troops fought magnificently to accomplish it. Had this happened, the European war might well have been shortened by months. While the Nijmegen bridges were secured, however, it was impossible to hold out at Arnhem, and finally the remnants of the Allied Airborne Division were withdrawn. In the picture a "Liberator" aircraft is swooping low over the Dutch countryside to drop supplies to paratroops below. The ground is covered with gliders and collapsed parachutes. More parachutes, loaded with supplies, are seen dropping slowly towards earth.

GLIDERS LAND ON DUTCH FIELDS. The landing of Allied airborne forces continued steadily during 18-19 September. Considerable reinforcements of men, equipment and stores were flown into Holland, and all were strongly protected by large numbers of British and U.S. fighters and fighter bombers. The conception and execution of the whole airborne operation must rank as one of the major events in military history. In contrast

with the previous airborne landings in France, Italy, and North Africa, parachutists and glider-borne infantry had all
to be dropped in pin-pointed areas to make sure that troops were concentrated in strength at or very near vital
objectives. Each soldier carried with him a detailed map of the particular area in which he was to operate. The
picture on these pages shows the gliders covering the Dutch fields after some of the first landings had been made.

EPIC OF ARNHEM

Through eight days and nights the men of the First Airborne Army fought on around Arnhem. It was a truly heroic struggle against quite overwhelming odds, for the Germans had concentrated considerable forces in the confined area. Moreover, the bad weather that developed soon after the landings made it quite impossible to keep the airborne troops supplied from the air; though, needless to say, the Allied air crews worked wonders whenever there was the slightest opportunity to do so. Diving in at recklessly low levels, many aircraft were shot down by enemy guns. But the isolated troops fought bravely on, sometimes with only jack-knives and pistols to defend themselves. For several days many of them were fighting without food and practically no water. Finally the order came to withdraw, and out of the 8,000 men who had been dropped around Arnhem only about one-third of their number were successfully brought back. Many of the wounded fell prisoners to the Germans. Above, men of (C) Company of the Border Regiment waiting to repulse the enemy less than 100 yards away; left, engaging the Germans with 3-in. mortars; top right, an airborne soldier in action with Sten gun; bottom right, some survivors of Arnhem.

BRITISH WATCH ON THE RHINE. Nijmegen Bridge over the Waal, Lower Rhine, was successfully taken by airborne forces and British Second Army troops after grim fighting. Despite heavy attacks from the Luftwaffe on 28 September, the enemy failed to cut this vital bridgehead into the Eindhoven corridor. A British soldier is seen on patrol in a command post guarding the bridge. Note picture of Hitler in lower right corner.

Plan of airborne attack

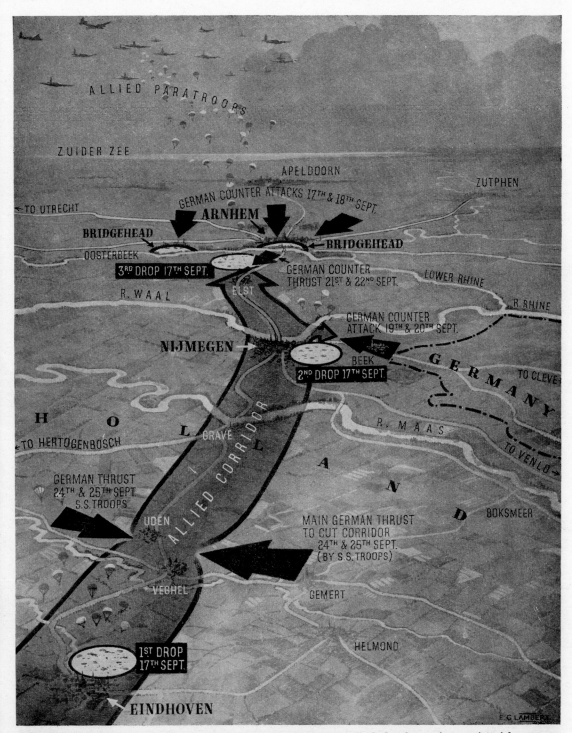

ACTION AT ARNHEM. This map, specially drawn for the book by E. G. Lambert, gives a pictorial summary of the famous airborne action at and around Arnhem. It shows the three main points where the Allied paratroops were dropped on 17-18 September, a link being made between airborne forces at Eindhoven and Nijmegen the following days. Chief enemy thrusts against Allied corridor were made on 24-25 September, when that corridor was greatly strengthened. Local German attacks against Arnhem and Nijmegen bridgeheads are also shown.

FIGHTING FOR THE ARNHEM BRIDGE. Some of the most bitter fighting of the war occurred at the approaches to the vital bridge at Arnhem. Although the 1st Airborne Division battled against quite overwhelming odds here, suffering a great many casualties both in killed and wounded, they succeeded in inflicting heavy losses on the

enemy. Their stand at Arnhem will take a shining place in the records of gallant deeds in all wars. This special drawing by Charles Cundall gives a most vivid impression of the scene at the approaches to the bridge at Arnhem during the climax of the battle, when men of the 1st Airborne Division so distinguished themselves.

BRITISH LIBERATE EINDHOVEN. On 19 September troops of the British Second Army entered Eindhoven, the first large city of Holland to be set free. They received a tremendous welcome from the inhabitants. Although the famous Philips radio works had been badly hit in previous R.A.F. attacks, the town itself was found practically undamaged. Above, British lorries passing through a street in Eindhoven (by permission of "The Times"); top right, welcoming the liberators; bottom right, clearing an enemy road block near the Belgian-Dutch frontier.

Great haul of prisoners

FALL OF BREST. On 19 September all enemy resistance ceased in Brest, the important French Atlantic seaport which the Germans had used as a U-boat base for more than four years. Nearly 11,000 prisoners were taken, including the German naval commander, Admiral Kahler. This brought the total of prisoners captured during the siege of forty-six days to more than 35,000. Pictures show: top left, a U.S. tank destroyer firing at point-blank range to clear a side street; bottom left, German women among prisoners; above, more prisoners from Brest.

RIMINI CAPTURED. On 21 September, after very bitter fighting, the important Adriatic coast town of Rimini fell to Greek infantry and Canadian tanks of the Eighth Army. Although the main German forces had already quitted the town, some stubborn pockets of enemy resistance still remained to be cleared. Infantrymen are seen above during a house-to-house mopping-up in the centre of Rimini. On the left an Allied soldier is taking quick cover behind a lorry during a sudden enemy counter-attack on the road between Rimini and Bologna.

END OF SIEGE AT CALAIS

On 1 October the German commander of Calais, Colonel Schoerner, surrendered unconditionally to the Canadian forces. A few hours later the rest of the garrison ceased resistance, and Calais had been freed. With the capture of this town all the French Channel ports opposite the south-east coast of England had now been liberated, with the single exception of Dunkirk. Earlier a truce had been granted to the German commander of Calais to allow the evacuation of the townspeople. After this there followed a terrific bombardment by the Canadians, using both light and heavy artillery. R.A.F. Bomber Command also took part in the assault, dropping over 11,000 tons of bombs from very low altitudes. Altogether nearly 8,000 prisoners were taken at Calais. By clearing the enemy from this part of the French coast, the last of the German cross-Channel guns were silenced. Pictures show: left, one of many buildings ablaze as the Canadians entered the town; above, civilians being evacuated; right, a Canadian rifleman on guard outside the former Nazi headquarters in the centre of the town.

ALLIES LAND IN GREECE

On the night of 4-5 October units of Allied Land Forces (Adriatic) landed on the mainland of Greece and entered the town of Patras, in the northern Peloponnesus. Other units made landings on several of the Greek Islands, and all these very successful land operations were closely supported by strong detachments of the Balkan Air Force and the Royal Navy. Paratroops had been dropped in Greece a few days before the landings from the sea, and R.A.F. "Spitfires" had also touched down on Greek airfields without meeting any opposition from the Germans. In response to an appeal sent out by the Greek Resistance Movement, local citizens gave willing assistance with the making of emergency landing-strips for Allied aircraft. After a great welcome from the people of Patras, where about 1,600 remaining Germans were taken prisoners, the Allies pushed on towards Corinth, liberated on 8 October. By this time the Germans were beating a hasty retreat out of Greece, leaving extensive demolitions behind them. British patrols were able to push across the Corinth Canal without making further contact with the enemy. Athens, the Greek capital, was freed by a British Commando force on 13 October. Picture shows the Mayor of Patras (bareheaded and on horseback) being greeted by a fellow partisan as he rides through the thronged streets.

Enemy launch rocket

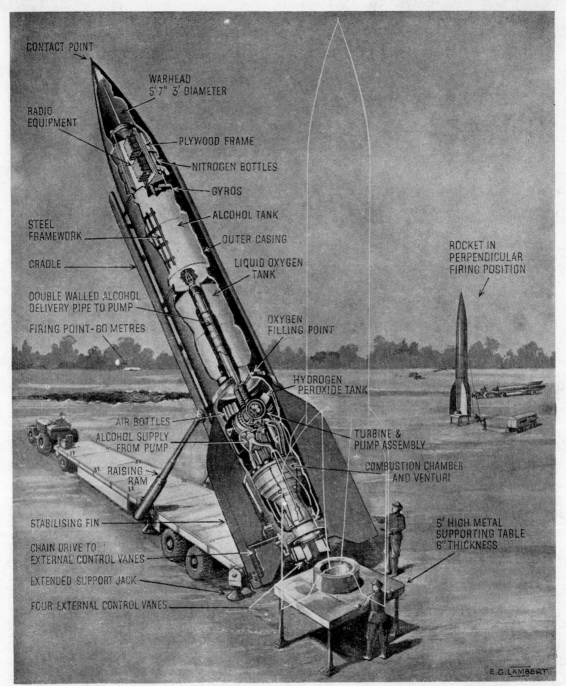

CONTACT POINT

WARHEAD
5'7" 3' DIAMETER

RADIO
EQUIPMENT

PLYWOOD FRAME

NITROGEN BOTTLES

GYROS

ALCOHOL TANK

STEEL
FRAMEWORK

OUTER CASING

CRADLE

LIQUID OXYGEN
TANK

DOUBLE WALLED ALCOHOL
DELIVERY PIPE TO PUMP

FIRING POINT-60 METRES

OXYGEN
FILLING POINT

HYDROGEN
PEROXIDE TANK

AIR BOTTLES

ALCOHOL SUPPLY
FROM PUMP

TURBINE &
PUMP ASSEMBLY

RAISING
RAM

COMBUSTION CHAMBER
AND VENTURI

STABILISING FIN

CHAIN DRIVE TO
EXTERNAL CONTROL VANES

EXTENDED SUPPORT JACK

FOUR EXTERNAL CONTROL VANES

ROCKET IN
PERPENDICULAR
FIRING POSITION

5' HIGH METAL
SUPPORTING TABLE
6" THICKNESS

E.G. LAMBERT

GERMAN ROCKET-BOMB. Early in October the enemy began in earnest their rocket-bomb attacks against southern England, and these continued through the autumn and winter months. While the rocket was much less accurate than the flying-bomb, it was a more deadly weapon, making a crater 30 ft. deep and causing damage over a wide area. Much larger than the flying-bomb, its warhead contained 2,000 lb. of explosive. Its flight could not be intercepted and, moreover, the small platforms used as launching sites were hard to destroy by bombing. Most of the rockets which fell in England were fired from sites in Holland. The weapon had a range of about 200 miles and ascended 60 or 70 miles during flight. This special drawing illustrates detailed construction of the rocket-bomb, and shows how it is raised into firing position. Right, rescue work after rocket incident in London.

HEAVY AIR ATTACKS IN BURMA. During October many powerful blows were struck against important Japanese communications and supply routes in Burma in support of the advancing Fourteenth Army by the Strategic Air Force of Eastern Air Command. The picture above shows a direct hit from an R.A.F. "Liberator" bursting on enemy railway yards at Ye, near the main line running from Bangkok to Rangoon. Right, leaflets being showered from one of the attacking aircraft after a heavy raid on an enemy-held railway station at Pak Nem Phau.

KING GEORGE VISITS THE WESTERN FRONT. On 11 October His Majesty the King flew across the Channel to make a five-day tour of the battlefields of France, Belgium, and Holland and visit the Allied forces in the front line. In the course of this tour he motored more than 200 miles in a single day in order to confer the K.C.B. on Lieutenant-General Omar Bradley, famous Commander of the American 12th Army Group. The King travelled about the battlefields mostly in a jeep and slept each night in an Army caravan as the guest of Field-Marshal Montgomery. He received a warm welcome not only from the fighting men but also from crowds of civilians in the liberated towns and villages through which he passed. Pictures on these pages, taken during His Majesty's visit to the Western Front, show: the King enjoying a joke with General Eisenhower (with them Lieutenant-General Omar Bradley and General Hodges); right, leaving the British headquarters with Field-Marshal Montgomery.

SUCCESSES IN BURMA. During October British and Indian troops of the Fourteenth Army made good progress in Burma after months of heavy fighting for the important Tiddim Road amid difficult conditions. Tiddim itself, pre-war centre of the Chin Hills territory, was captured on 19 October after Japanese resistance on the steep "Chocolate Staircase" had collapsed, and their defences covering the northern approach to the town were smashed under heavy air attacks. Above, Indian troops of Fifth Division on Kennedy Peak, an 8,000-ft. height in the Chin Hills beyond Tiddim; top right, Royal Scots Fusiliers seeking out enemy snipers in a Burmese village; bottom right, another party of Royal Scots Fusiliers crossing a swirling stream in the jungle with rifles, spades and bagpipes.

FALL OF AACHEN. After more than one week of fierce street battles, the German city of Aachen fell to the American First Army on 20 October. Ten days earlier the Americans had presented a "surrender or die" ultimatum to the German garrison, but as no reply was received the attack on the city was resumed. Besides terrific artillery bombardments, Aachen was continuously dive-bombed and strafed by wave after wave of Allied bombers. By the time that the end came the place was a heap of ruins and rubble. Above, U.S. envoys carry surrender ultimatum to the Germans; top right, German civilians leave; below, a suburb of Aachen as it looked after the bombing and violent street battles were over and the city was forced to capitulate.

U.S. TROOPS LAND IN PHILIPPINES. On 20 October General MacArthur announced that in a major amphibious operation his forces had seized the eastern coast of Leyte Island in the Philippines, 2,500 miles from Milne Bay (New Guinea) where the offensive in the Pacific had begun sixteen months previously. The place selected

for the landings, midway between Luzon and Mindanao, caught the Japanese unawares and split their forces in the Philippines into two. Landings were preceded by devastating air and sea bombardments, and U.S. casualties were far lighter than anticipated. Joyous Filipinos are seen mingling with their liberators on Leyte.

RECONQUEST OF THE PHILIPPINES. This map, specially drawn by S. J. Turner, F.R.G.S., shows stages in the recapture of the Philippines which began with the landings on Leyte in the south-west. This large group of Pacific islands, with their numerous airfields and good naval bases, form a strategic key to all future operations designed to carry the war into Japan itself. The landings on Leyte were the greatest of the Pacific war to date. In the picture on the opposite page General MacArthur is seen talking to native Filipino warriors.

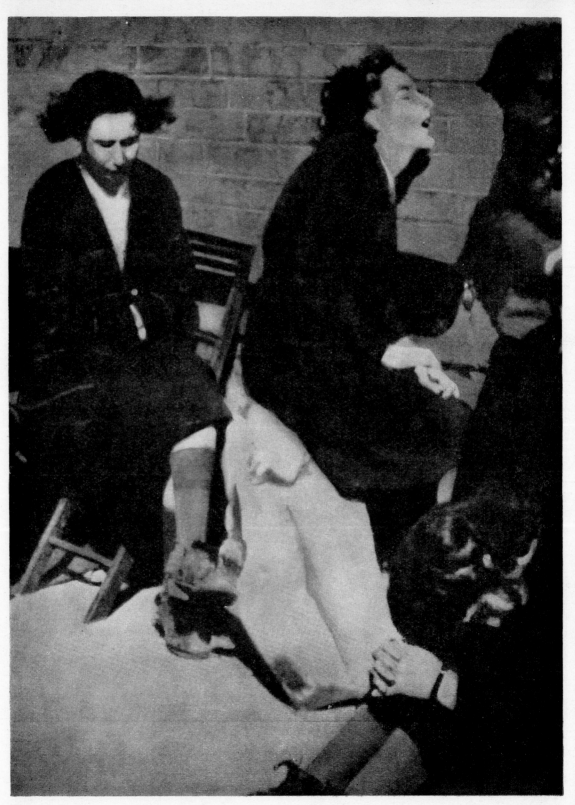

TRAGIC STRUGGLE IN WARSAW

On 21 October the heroic defenders of Warsaw fired their last shots in the struggle to seize the city from the German troops in occupation. For over two months the Polish Patriot Army had waged a gallant fight, but the exhaustion of all weapons and food supplies compelled them to cease resistance. Hope of relief from outside vanished when attempts by the Red Army, with Polish formations, to cross the Vistula failed. The pictures here show: left, some of the starving civilians of Warsaw after the rising; above, Germans blindfold Polish delegates just arrived at their headquarters to discuss the terms of surrender; right, a party of Polish patriots being marched away after the capitulation of city was signed.

RED ARMY INVADES EAST PRUSSIA. On 23 October the Soviet invasion of East Prussia was announced by Marshal Stalin in an Order of the Day addressed to General Chernyakhovsky. For some days previously, however, the German broadcasts had been giving the long-expected news of the Russian advance into Reich territory. Supported with massed blows by artillery and aircraft, powerful Soviet forces broke through deeply

staggered enemy defences covering the frontier and entered East Prussia to a depth of nearly twenty miles on an eighty-five-mile front. Many powerful strong-points were overtaken on the first day during bitter fighting, and a total of 400 places were occupied by the Red Army. The advance made good progress despite fierce German resistance and counter-attacks, though by 30 October it had been slowed down. Above, Red Army tanks advance.

BATTLE FOR HERTOGENBOSCH. On 26 October the old Dutch town of Hertogenbosch (Bois-le-Duc) was at last cleared of the Germans by General Dempsey's troops, in their steady advance across the bogged countryside of Holland. For several days there had been some heavy street fighting in the town, where groups of enemy troops were resisting stubbornly. British flame-throwers played an important part in covering the final British

infantry attack. Fortunately, the fine Gothic cathedral was left undamaged. Pictures show: top left, Royal Engineers crossing Dommel Canal south of Hertogenbosch; top right, British troops advancing towards town; bottom left, infantrymen take cover in street doorways while searching for snipers; centre, a party of British infantry waits to move forward; bottom right, Dutch civilian removing children from scene of street battles.

GERMAN FAMILIES BECOME REFUGEES. As the war was carried into the Reich itself, it was now the turn of German civilians to experience something of what their Fuehrer had mercilessly inflicted upon millions of innocent people elsewhere in Europe. The pictures on these pages show German families on the move as Allied progress overwhelms their towns and villages. Above, a German farmer pushing a loaded wheelbarrow; top right, a typical German housewife taking her belongings to safety; bottom right, civilians leaving fighting area.

GERMAN HEADQUARTERS BOMBED. On 31 October a daring low-level attack was made by "Mosquitoes" of R.A.F. Tactical Air Force on the Gestapo headquarters housed in the University of Aarhus, Denmark. Two adjoining four-storey buildings formed the target, and to obtain accuracy in bombing a model was specially made for the crews. Photograph above shows two of the "Mosquitoes" over the target with bombs falling; pictures on the opposite page, taken by a reconnaissance aircraft from almost roof-top height, show the success of the attack.

BRITISH AND CANADIANS INVADE WALCHEREN

On 1 November British Commandos and British and Canadian infantry landed at Flushing and Westkapelle on the island of Walcheren. This operation was launched in order to clear the enemy from the approaches to the port of Antwerp, the use of which was vital to the Allied armies fighting on the Western front. The Flushing force crossed the Scheldt estuary in assault craft, and although enemy fire from shore defences was less fierce than anticipated, many submerged obstacles caused the loss of some landing-craft. After very stiff fighting ashore British and Canadian troops had cleared most of Flushing by nightfall. Although the Royal Marine Commandos met deadly opposition at Westkapelle, and many landing-craft were sunk, they charged ashore through a gap in the dyke, captured three of the biggest enemy batteries, and soon established a firm bridgehead. Pictures show: left, tank landing-craft approaching beach at Westkapelle; bottom left, British Commandos advancing along waterfront at Flushing with shells bursting ahead; bottom right, evacuating wounded at Flushing.

BRITISH ENTER SALONIKA. On 5 November British Commandos landed by sea at the important Greek seaport of Salonika.

ALLIED NAVAL VICTORY IN PACIFIC. On 22 October a great five-day naval battle was begun in the Philippine area. A crushing defeat was inflicted upon the enemy who lost more than sixty warships, sunk or damaged. U.S. Navy losses were comparatively light, a small aircraft carrier, two escort carriers, two destroyers and a destroyer-escort going down. By the middle of November remnants of the Japanese fleet had sought refuge in home waters. The picture shows one of the U.S. escort carriers, the "St. Lo." in flames just before she sank.

MR. CHURCHILL IN PARIS. On 11 November the British Prime Minister, accompanied by Mr. Eden, took part in the Armistice Day celebrations in Paris at the invitation of General de Gaulle. After laying a wreath on the Unknown Soldier's tomb at the Arc de Triomphe, Mr. Churchill and General de Gaulle, followed by Mr. Eden, M. Bidault and other British and French leaders, walked down the famous Champs-Élysées to the thunderous cheers of "Vive Churchill!" and "Vive de Gaulle!" In the photograph Mr. Churchill is seen acknowledging crowds.

ALLIED BOMBERS SMASH GERMAN RAILWAYS. During November British and American bomber forces continued their relentless day and night attacks on German communications. Among the chief targets were railway marshalling yards, important junctions, viaducts and tunnels. On 16 November the greatest bomb load ever dropped on Germany to date—more than 5,600 tons—wiped out the big rail centres of Duren and Heinsberg in the Rhineland. Pictures show: above, 9th Air Force "Marauder" aircraft dropping their bombs on the marshalling yards at Enskirchen; top right, rocket-firing aircraft attack goods train; below, a bombed viaduct in Germany.

INSIDE NAZI MURDER CAMP

During November the advancing Allies overran a notorious concentration camp used by the Germans at Vught, in south-west Holland. It is estimated that more than 13,500 innocent men, women and children were cruelly tortured and murdered here during the four years that the Nazis were in charge. This camp was typical of so many built throughout the German-occupied countries and in the Reich itself, and the pictures illustrate some of its horrors. Left, a gallows on which many Dutch patriots were executed; right, a hot-air torture chamber, showing inlet pipes; below, an oven where thousands of bodies were burnt.

Air war against Japan

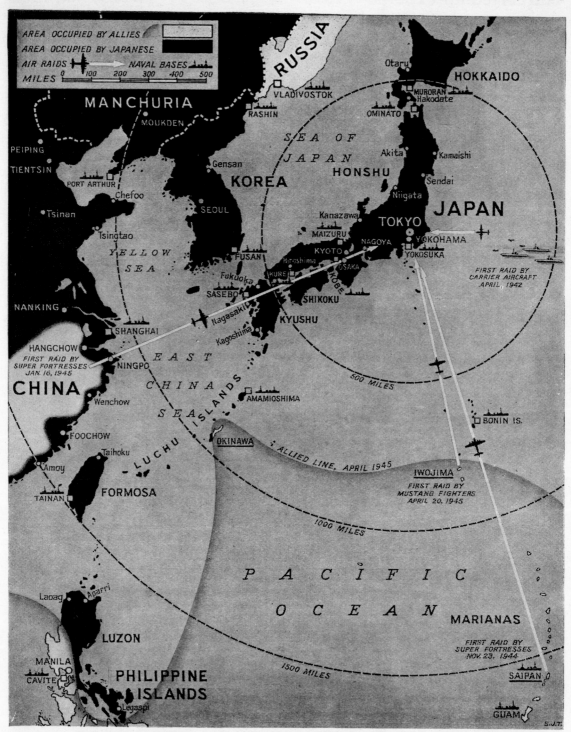

BOMBING OF JAPANESE CITIES. During the autumn and winter of 1944-45 increasingly heavy raids were made on Tokyo and other large Japanese cities by American "Super-Fortresses," flying from recently won island bases in the Pacific and, latterly, from bases on the Chinese mainland. Attacks from carrier-borne aircraft, which had made the earliest raids on Japan, were continued as well. The pictorial map above, specially drawn for this book by S. J. Turner, F.R.G.S., shows how this Far East bombing offensive was mounting by the early months of 1945.

Chinese helped by air power

AIR SUPPLIES FOR CHINA. While the tremendous increase in American air power throughout the Far East took the war to the very heart of the Japanese homeland, it brought much-needed assistance and relief to the valiant native armies of China. Powerful air forces flew from distant bases in India and the liberated parts of Burma to drop ammunition, equipment and supplies to the Chinese. Here is a parachute load on its way down.

BRITISH ADVANCE INTO GERMANY. At dawn on 18 November a powerful assault was begun in Germany, north and south of Geilenkirchen, by the British Second Army which had been switched to this front from Holland and was fighting side by side with the Americans under General Dempsey. The British and Americans developed a pincers movement round Geilenkirchen, and this important German strong-point before the Rhine fell to the combined attack on 19 November. War correspondents described the place as a "ghost town," for it had been reduced to rubble by heavy air and artillery bombardment. Of the town's normal population of 20,000 not more than about 300 remained. The Germans shelled and mortared Geilenkirchen after its occupation by the Allies. The picture shows British infantry amid the desolation of Bauchem, a few miles from Geilenkirchen

LIBERATION OF STRASBOURG. On 19 November the French First Army launched a big attack from the Vosges to the Swiss frontier, taking 10,000 prisoners. Next day it captured Belfort and reached the Rhine south of Mulhouse. Meanwhile the U.S. Seventh Army was advancing towards Strasbourg. This great French city, capital of Alsace, was actually liberated by the French 2nd Armoured Division under General Leclerc. On the evening of 23 November the French flag was again flying over Strasbourg's famous cathedral, which had been badly damaged by the enemy. This victory brought both the French and Americans to the bridge across the Rhine opposite the German town of Kehl. It threatened still more the bulk of the German forces in the Vosges, who were already menaced by French armour driving northwards from Mulhouse. A scene in Strasbourg after its liberation is shown in the picture above. A street is littered with torn and trampled-on "swastikas."

Civil strife breaks out

FIGHTING IN ATHENS

On 3 December fighting broke out in Athens after EAM (Left Wing) representatives in the Greek Government had resigned rather than sign the decree disbanding all armed resistance forces. Next day their supporters demonstrated and clashed with the police and civil war followed. British troops were ordered by General Scobie to restore peace, but without success. After ELAS (the rebel army) had attacked the British naval headquarters, heavy fighting followed for some days. The pictures show: left, British tanks entering EAM building; below, prisoners coming away; top right, British paratroops in street fighting; bottom right, ELAS supporters in the street fighting.

BRITAIN'S HOME GUARD STANDS DOWN. On 3 December more than 7,000 representative members of the Home Guard from every part of the country gathered in London for the final parade before H.M. he King, who took the salute in Hyde Park. Local parades were also held in almost every town and village of Britain to mark the officia. Stand Down. Many of the men in the London celebration had served since the Home Guard was formed as the Local Defence Volunteers 'n May, 1940. The King, in a special message, said: "The Home Guard has reached the end of its long tour of duty under arms. You have earned in full measure the gratitude of your country." The picture shows one of the Home Guard contingents marching down Piccadilly towards Hyde Park.

Volkssturm marches out

GERMANY'S VOLKSSTURM PREPARES TO FIGHT. While the main task of the Home Guard in Britain was over, the swift advance of the Allied armies into the Reich made necessary the formation of a German "People's Army." In the middle of October, when Germany was already being invaded from east and west, Hitler had delivered an emergency proclamation calling on all male Germans between sixteen and sixty, able to carry arms, to prepare themselves for the defence of the Fatherland. Volkssturm units were hastily formed in many towns and villages, each under the command of reliable Nazi party officials. Some were provided with uniforms, but most wore civilian clothes with an arm-band bearing the German emblem. Above, a Volkssturm parade in Berlin.

GERMAN COUNTER-OFFENSIVE IN WEST. At dawn on 16 December the Germans, under von Rundstedt, suddenly launched a full-scale offensive against the U.S. First Army in the Ardennes. The enemy's attack was the biggest since Normandy, and the Luftwaffe appeared in greater strength than at any time since D-Day. Rundstedt's plan, which had been prepared in secret, was to capture the vital communications centre of Liége, and from there drive the Allies back to the coast. By 20 December the enemy had driven a twenty-five-mile wedge into the American positions and had thrown thirteen to fifteen divisions into the offensive. But although much initial success was gained, German losses proved very heavy in this all-out bid to stem the Allies west of the Rhine. The map shows the extent of the enemy's drive into Belgium. On the right, enemy troops in action.

HARD FIGHTING
IN WEST

On 21 December it was revealed that the Germans had thrust thirty miles into Belgium and had cut the important Liége-Bastogne road only eighteen miles south of Liége. Next day Allied H.Q. announced that the enemy's offensive had been checked; at i's deepest penetration it reached Laroche, fourteen miles north-west of Bastogne. In some of the greatest armoured battles fought in the West, the enemy had already lost 200 tanks. So far the bad weather had helped Rundstedt, but on 23 December the skies suddenly cleared and allowed a force of more than 4,000 Allied aircraft to blast enemy positions and communications. By 27 December Rundstedt's drive to the Meuse had been halted. Top, Allied forces move up to counter-attack; left, dead Germans in wood near Liesneux. The dramatic picture on the opposite page was taken as a German pillbox was blown up by U.S. Army engineers.

ATHENS CONFERENCE

On 24 December Mr. Churchill and Mr. Eden, accompanied by diplomatic officials and military advisers, arrived in Athens and there called a conference of the conflicting parties in the Greek political crisis in an effort to bring about peace. The conference, presided over by Archbishop Damaskinos, met on 26 December in a room lighted by hurricane lamps. It was attended by the British representatives, M. Papandreou, E.A.M. and E.L.A.S. delegates, and representatives from all the Greek political parties. The conference resumed on the following day when the question of a Regency for Greece was discussed. Later, it was agreed to appoint Archbishop Damaskinos as Regent. On the left the conference is seen in session. Around the table, left to right, are Mr. Eden, Mr. Churchill, Archbishop Damaskinos, Field-Marshal Alexander, Mr. Harold Macmillan (Minister Resident Allied H.Q. Mediterranean), and General Scobie (G.O.C. in Greece). Above, Mr. Churchill is seen with Archbishop Damaskinos.

SIEGE OF BASTOGNE

On 27 December the 4th Armoured Division of General Patton's Third Army, after fighting its way across difficult country, made contact with the gallant defenders of Bastogne. Thus ended one of the most heroic episodes of the war. For eight days and nine nights the American 101st Airborne Division, supported by a unit of the 10th Armoured Division, held out against the enemy which encircled them. Under their commander, Brigadier-General McAuliffe, they repulsed powerful assaults by seven or eight German divisions, killed hundreds of the enemy, destroyed 144 tanks, and took 700 to 800 prisoners. Their undaunted bravery contributed much to the success of all subsequent operations against the German salient, for Bastogne was a vital centre of communications. Early in the siege the defenders lost their only field hospital, and hundreds of wounded had to be tended in makeshift hospitals with only a handful of doctors until weather conditions made it possible for airborne supplies to be flown in. On 22 December the Germans sent emissaries under a white flag to General McAuliffe demanding surrender. In reply, the general sent back a large envelope containing a sheet of paper bearing the single word, "Nuts." Pressure on the garrison was relieved when, between 23-26 December, the 1st Allied Airborne Army flew in 842 "Dakotas" which parachuted supplies and ammunition. Picture on the right shows refugees plodding through Bastogne.

ALLIES LAUNCH COUNTER-ATTACK

By 29 December some substantial progress had been made by troops of the First Army along the northern side of the German salient, where the enemy had begun a major withdrawal. Among several important towns recaptured by the Allies were Manhay, Grandmenil and Humain, to the south-west of Marche. Even greater advances, however, were made along the southern flank, where forces under General Patton had covered more than sixteen miles in under six days to relieve the American Airborne Division besieged in Bastogne. During the early days of January, powerful new offensives were launched by both the First and Third Armies and much ground was recovered. It was announced that during the first sixteen days of the German counter-offensive in the Ardennes, the enemy lost something approaching 20,000 men in prisoners alone, more than 400 tanks, 650 aircraft, and numerous supply vehicles. Pictures show: top, a force of Allied artillerymen press on through the snow in camouflaged suits; below, troops of an American armoured division move up towards the battle line through snow.

PROGRESS IN THE ARDENNES. In early January heavy snow on the Western Front made fighting in the Ardennes salient difficult. Tanks and vehicles were frequently ditched or stranded on ice-bound roads. Nevertheless, good progress was made by the Allies. On 11 January Anglo-American troops under Field-Marshal Montgomery's command captured Laroche. This was one of the German key-points and communication centres. Above, an American tank moves along an icy road; top right, gun-site in snow; below, in a newly won town.

HOUFFALIZE RECAPTURED. On 16 January the American First Army entered the town of Houffalize in Belgium, from which the enemy had pulled out when his position threatened to become untenable. With the Allies back in this town, in and about which there had been most bitter fighting, the German salient in the

Ardennes was virtually rubbed out and replaced by a more or less north to south front line. Houffalize was found to be nothing but a ruined shell when it was at last wrested from the Germans, and the picture on these pages gives a very vivid impression of the destruction. Before U.S. troops could advance bridges had to be built.

GREATEST SOVIET OFFENSIVE BEGINS. On 12 January powerful Russian forces under Marshal Koniev struck the long-expected blow from their Vistula bridgehead, west of Sandomierz. Within two days the main German defences in Poland had been shattered, as the Red Army surged forward some twenty-five miles on a front of forty miles. On 15 January the great city of Kielice, with 400 other places, was captured, and Koniev's armies were driving rapidly towards the frontier of German Silesia. This was reached only three days later. Meanwhile, to the north, great forces under Marshal Zhukov were also unleashed on two fronts south of Warsaw.

After three days' fighting they broke through deeply staggered enemy defences and linked into one solid front. Warsaw fell on 17 January. Yet farther north, Marshal Rokossovsky joined the general offensive in a full-scale assault over the Narev river with the objective of outflanking East Prussia. Right along the entire Eastern Front more than 1,500,000 Russians were engaged in the final all-out push against Nazi Germany. Four leading commanders of the Red Army are shown here. Top left, Marshal Rokossovsky; below, Marshal Konieve; top right, Marshal Malinovsky; below, Marshal Zhukov. Centre pictures, Red tanks in newly captured cities.

German prisoners taken

RUSSIANS ADVANCE IN CZECHOSLOVAKIA. On 15 January troops of the Fourth Ukrainian Front began an offensive in the Carpathians. Advancing through roadless mountains and forests, they captured many enemy strong-points on Czechoslovak territory. A week or so later the town of Poprad, on the railway line to Bratislava and Vienna, was captured, and the vital centre of Novy Targ also fell to the Red Army. Left, German prisoners in Czechoslovakia; top right, Red Army troops go forward; below, Soviet heavy guns move up to the front.

RED ARMY SURGES WESTWARDS. Greater even than the advances made by the Russian armies during the summer of 1944 were the spectacular offensives of the 1944-45 winter campaign. The map on this page illustrates the speed and force of the Red Army's relentless drive into the very heart of Reich territory and finally to the German capital itself. The severance of East Prussia from the rest of Germany was one of the decisive blows which brought disaster to Nazi power in Eastern Europe. Opposite page: scenes during the Russian offensives.

Germans finally driven

RED ARMY LIBERATES WARSAW. On 17 January, after forcing a crossing of the Vistula south of the city, Marshal Zhukov's forces captured Warsaw, capital of Poland. Troops of the First Polish Army, with those of the First White Russian Front, were chosen to take part in the liberation. Soviet war correspondents who entered Warsaw described it as completely devastated with hardly a living soul to be seen. Most of the famous buildings and monuments had been ruthlessly destroyed by the enemy. Pictures above show some of the stricken inhabitants of Warsaw returning to their shattered streets and homes. Right, Polish soldiers march through Warsaw.

German dead after stree

FIGHTING IN EAST PRUSSIA. On 20 January, after a lull of nearly three months, heavy fighting was resumed in East Prussia. Soviet troops of the Third White Russian Front captured by storm the towns of Tilsit, Gross, Skaisgirren, Aulowohnen, Szillen and Kaukehmen. All these were important communication centres and powerful strong-points in the German defences covering Konigsberg. Tilsit, third largest town in East Prussia, fell as a result of the displacement of German forces protecting the town in an attempt to steady the hard-pressed defenders of Gumbinnen farther south. Many other big towns also fell in the great Russian double thrust into East Prussia by forces under Marshal Rokossovsky and General Chernyakhovsky. These included Allenstein

and Insterburg, the last-named being forty miles inside the German border. The Red Air Force, supporting the land armies, enjoyed complete air supremacy over the whole of East Prussia. In the last days of January there was bitter fighting for Konigsberg, capital of the German province, which was now completely encircled with every street ablaze. Dispatches from Moscow stated that more than 150,000 German refugees from other battle areas had taken refuge in the city, believing it to be beyond the reach of the Red Army. All of them had to live permanently in underground cellars for a great part of the town had been devastated by heavy artillery fire and bombing. Pictured above is a street in a captured East Prussian town scattered with many German dead.

RUSSIAN TROOPS ENTER SILESIA

On 21 January the invasion of German Silesia by Red Army troops of Marshal Koniev's command was greeted in Moscow by a salute of 20 salvos from 224 guns. The Russians broke through strongly fortified enemy defences on the south-east border of Germany and, entering Silesia on a front fifty-six miles long, captured the large towns of Kreuzburg, Rosenberg, Landsberg and Guttentag. All these were described as important communication centres and powerful strong-points in the defences covering the roads to Breslau. Further notable gains were made by the Red Army during the following days, and Germany was now faced with the loss of the rich Upper Silesian industrial basin where so many of her great war factories were located. Pictures on these pages show: top left, Soviet infantry dislodging some Germans from a strong-point while clearing a town; top right, Russian tanks passing through the industrial town of Gleiwitz, Upper Silesia; below, Soviet artillery in action while fighting for Breslau.

CRIMEA CONFERENCE

On 3 February began the historic meetings between Mr. Churchill, President Roosevelt and Marshal Stalin in the Livadia Palace at Yalta, in the Crimea. On the previous day Mr. Churchill and President Roosevelt met in Malta and, after conferences, flew thence by air to a Soviet airport in the Crimea, where they were met by Marshal Stalin and M. Molotov. All three leaders were accompanied at the Yalta meetings, which lasted for eight days, by their respective Foreign Secretaries, Chiefs of Staff and other advisers. Most important of the many subjects under discussion at this, the most momentous of all the "Big Three" meetings that had so far taken place, were the military plans for the final defeat of Germany. The conference agreed on the enforcement of the "unconditional surrender" terms for the aggressors in Europe and plans for the occupation of a separate zone of Germany by forces of each of the three powers. Many of the problems involved in establishing a secure peace were also discussed by the great war leaders in a spirit of mutual accord. The results of the Crimea Conference were made known to the world on 12 February in simultaneous broadcasts from London, Washington and Moscow. In every land the news was greeted with whole-hearted approval, for it was felt that the meetings had paved the way for the creation of a long and satisfactory peace. The photograph of the three world leaders reproduced here was taken in the grounds of the Livadia Palace during the Conference. Left to right, Mr. Churchill (wearing a Cossack cap), President Roosevelt and Marshal Stalin.

FRENCH ARMY FREES COLMAR. On 2 February troops of the French Army fought their way into the centre of Colmar, third largest city in the province of Alsace. This victory sealed the fate of the German Nineteenth Army remaining in the so-called "Colmar Pocket," for although it was strongly resisting on the southern flank, to the north and west of Mulhouse, its chief route of supply or withdrawal had been cut by French troops astride the Colmar-Neuf Brisach road. Dispatches sent by war correspondents reported that the whole German position in Alsace was rapidly breaking up. After some fierce fighting in the streets of Colmar, the city's population turned out to give their liberators a most enthusiastic welcome. Here, units of the French Armoured Division are seen passing along the Avenue de la Republique during the victory celebrations in Colmar.

CLEVE OCCUPIED

On 12 February Cleve, a northern bastion of the Siegfried Line, fell to Scottish troops of the Canadian First Army. During the attack, led by "Churchill" flame-throwing tanks, many nests of snipers were overcome and several hundred prisoners taken. Formerly a picturesque medieval town with a pre-war population of nearly 25,000, Cleve was completely destroyed by the fighting and the preceding air bombardments. More than 700 R.A.F. "Lancasters" and "Halifaxes" made their heaviest night attack on German troops and supplies in Cleve on 7-8 February. Left, Cleve after its capture; above, British tanks move up to support the infantry clearing snipers' nests in the devastated town.

FALL OF BUDAPEST

On 13 February, after a siege which had lasted seven weeks, the Red Army completed their occupation of Budapest, the Hungarian capital. The Germans had fiercely contested every yard of the city, which was a strategically important bastion in the enemy's defences on the approaches to Vienna. Nevertheless, as the Soviet ring closed ever more tightly around Budapest, German losses mounted rapidly; indeed they proved to be the heaviest suffered by the enemy in any single battle of the war, exceeding even those at Stalingrad. Altogether the Red Army killed over 49,000 enemy troops and took over 110,000 German and Hungarian prisoners, including General Pfeffer-Wildenbruch, German commander of the Budapest garrison. During the fighting the enemy destroyed some of the city's finest buildings, blew up the Danube bridges and murdered large numbers of civilians. Left, street fighting in Budapest; bottom left, Soviet A.A. gunners in action in a city square; below, Soviet artillerymen pound the enemy from a captured suburb of the Hungarian capital.

RED ARMY ADVANCES BEYOND ODER. In mid-February powerful Soviet forces under Marshal Koniev crossed the River Oder and broke through strong enemy defences on the western bank. In four days the Russians advanced thirty-seven miles, widened their front to over one hundred miles, and took many strong-points, including the famous manufacturing town of Liegnitz, thirty-five miles north-west of Breslau. By 14 February the city of Neusalz had been reached, some forty miles farther on, and Marshal Koniev's troops now held 150 miles of the

upper and middle Oder beyond the upper Silesian industrial basin. By these spectacular advances the Red Army had overrun most of the wooded country between the Bober and Queis Rivers in twenty-four hours and smashed desperate German attempts to make a stand on the Bober before the big industrial town of Gorlitz, fifty miles east of Dresden. Top left, Soviet tommy-gunners fighting; bottom left, column of prisoners recross the Oder to rear of Russian lines; top right, long-range guns of Red Army in action; bottom right, Soviet troops march westwards.

BATTLE FOR GOCH

On 21 February Scottish and Welsh troops fighting with the Canadian First Army, under the command of General Crerar, completed the occupation of the enemy's stronghold of Goch, south-east of the Reichswald Forest. Three nights previously, in a silent assault, Scottish infantry of the Canadian First had broken into this great fortress town, which guarded the northern flank of the Siegfried Line. After some very fierce house-to-house fighting, more than two-thirds of the place was in British hands. Such surprise was effected in the initial night attack that the commander of the German garrison, Colonel Paul Matussek, and his staff were captured while asleep in their beds. On 20 February Welsh troops, attacking from north of Goch, smashed their way through the factory district to link up with the Scottish troops in the centre of the town, which had been reduced to ruins. Even when the occupation of this German strong-point was virtually completed, several lively nests of enemy snipers continued to hold out in the shattered buildings. But they were quickly rounded up or wiped out by the British. An aerial view showing destruction in Goch is seen on left; above, a British soldier, screened by the wreckage of a house, keeps watch for snipers.

135

CROSSING THE ROER. On 23 February the U.S. First and Ninth Armies launched a powerful offensive across the Roer to the east of Aachen. The swift-moving river was crossed by infantry in "ducks" and assault craft and by pontoon bridges, the operation being made under cover of a smoke screen. Within three days a bridgehead on a twenty-eight-mile front was established, and Julich and Duren were taken. Left, one of the bridges built across the Roer by U.S. engineers smashed by German artillery; above, carrying supplies over the Roer.

LIBERATION OF MANILA. On 24 February, after a hard, three-weeks' battle, American troops completed the liberation of the Philippine capital. Although a great part of Manila had been captured early in the month, the Japanese continued fighting in the south of the city and created widespread havoc and destruction chiefly to deprive the Americans of any value from their gains. Extensive fires were started. Top left, dead Japanese in a street of Manila; bottom left, one of many streets in the city set ablaze by the enemy; above, U.S. transport enters Manila.

FALL OF COLOGNE. On 6 March the third largest city in Germany, and capital of the Rhineland, was captured by forces of the American First Army under General Hodges. After breaking through the strong outer defences, the Americans met but little opposition from the enemy garrison, and by nightfall they had reached the Rhine.

The great devastation caused by heavy Allied bombing in the centre of Cologne is illustrated in the photograph above; this also shows how the structure of the famous cathedral remained virtually intact despite its close proximity to the battle zone. The only bridge across Rhine left standing when city was taken was the Hohenzollern Bridge.

INSIDE CAPTURED COLOGNE

The utter destruction of the great industrial and commercial centres of Cologne was a foretaste of what the Anglo-American armies were to encounter everywhere in their victorious progress through the big cities of central Germany. It showed what an important contribution had been made by the British and American air forces in shortening the war in Europe. Pictures on this page show: left, German prisoners in front of Cologne Cathedral; below, a dramatic incident in a narrow street near the cathedral, when a U.S. soldier miraculously escaped death as his tank was blown up by the explosion of an enemy shell.

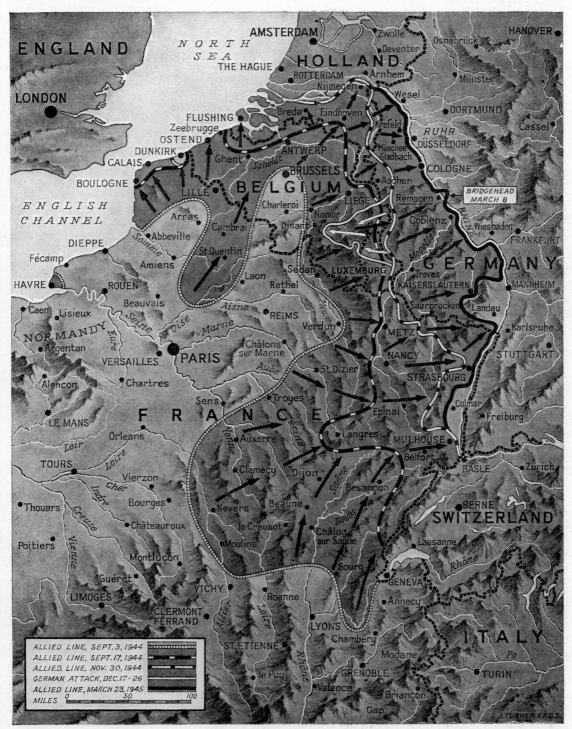

ADVANCE TO THE RHINE. This map shows stages of the great drive eastwards across France, Belgium and Holland to the Rhine from 3 September, 1944. Six Allied armies took part in the offensive under the supreme command of General Eisenhower. They were the British Second Army (including the Canadians), the American First, Third, Seventh and Ninth Armies, and the French First Army. The only serious check to the Allies was the German counter-attack in the Ardennes (17-26 December) which failed. First Rhine bridgehead gained on 8 March.

143

FIRST BRIDGEHEAD
OVER RHINE

On 8 March a bridgehead across the Rhine was established by the American First Army. The crossing was made over the Ludendorff railway bridge at Remagen between the cities of Bonn and Coblenz. The enemy had intended to blow up this bridge at four o'clock on the afternoon of 8 March, but by about 3.45 p.m. an American infantry patrol raced across to the far bank and two lieutenants hastily disconnected the fuses and charges. Within a few hours Allied tanks and infantry were pouring across the bridge and a firm bridgehead had been established on the east bank of the Rhine. The Germans were taken completely by surprise through this daring exploit, as a result of which large numbers of prisoners were captured and useful quantities of materials and supplies fell into American hands. Having realized his mistake the enemy began shelling the Ludendorff Bridge in an attempt to destroy it but these vain efforts failed to hinder the progress of the Allied build-up. On 9 March U.S. First Army headquarters announced that the attack across the Rhine was going well in face of light opposition, and that under cover of a powerful air "umbrella" strong reinforcements of men and material were crossing the bridge. Picture shows the Ludendorff Bridge under enemy fire at Remagen soon after it had been captured.

GERMAN RAILWAYS HEAVILY BOMBED. In the early days of March very powerful forces of British and American bombers roamed over Germany causing widespread havoc to the enemy's railways, oil storage depots and supply lines. Well over 1,000 aircraft were sent out each day, and their concentrated attacks with high-

explosive bombs on vital points in the German railway system speeded up the progress of the Anglo-American armies from the west and the Russian drive from the east. Repeated day and night attacks brought traffic to a complete standstill and damage was beyond repair. Above, a German goods train wrecked during an attack.

RHINE TOWNS CAPTURED. On 9 March the Americans entered the ancient town of Bonn, situated on the Rhine south of Cologne. The place had suffered heavy damage, though not on the scale of Cologne. Although the university was in ruins, the cathedral and the house where Beethoven was born escaped with only minor scars. Most of the citizens remained, having lived for weeks past in cellars. The First Army also captured Godesberg where Mr. Chamberlain flew to meet Hitler during the Czechoslovak crisis in 1938. Meanwhile U.S. troops of the First and Third Armies had linked up at a place on the Rhine south of Remagen, while other Third Army forces fought their way towards the great city of Coblenz, at the confluence of the Rhine and Moselle Rivers. Coblenz was captured on 17 March after hard street fighting. Left, U.S. troops in ruined Bonn; above, the American flag unfurled over Fort Ehrenbreitstein, Coblenz. It was last flown there during the occupation after 1918.

BATTLE FOR IWOJIMA. On 16 March all Japanese resistance ceased on Iwojima, the powerfully held Japanese bastion in the Volcano Islands. In announcing the victory Fleet-Admiral Nimitz described the four-week campaign as the costliest single action in the Pacific war. The enemy had held on to this tiny island with fanatical resistance and the fighting was without parallel in its ferocity. The total U.S. Marine casualties were 19,938, of whom 4,189

were killed, while the Japanese casualties amounted to more than 21,000, practically all of them killed. By the conquest of Iwojima the Allies gained a valuable air base within fighter range of the Japanese. Within a day or two after the fighting ended "Mustang" and "Black Widow" aircraft, capable of escorting "Super-Fortresses" to Tokyo, were already operating from the island. U.S. Marines are here seen on Iwojima beach ready to advance.

FALL OF MANDALAY. The last Japanese stronghold in the city of Mandalay, Fort Dufferin, fell to troops of the 19th Indian ("Dagger") Division at noon on 20 March. For ten days the enemy had fought bitterly to hold this fort, which, after resisting many attacks, was breached by "Mitchell" bombers using 2,000-lb. bombs. Five Burman refugees appeared with a white flag and surrendered the fort, from which the Japanese had already

fled. Soon afterwards the Union Jack was hoisted over it. The fall of Mandalay, second largest city in Burma, was a grand climax to the Fourteenth Army's difficult advance of 500 miles across the country. To mark the occasion H.M. the King sent a personal message of congratulation to Admiral Lord Louis Mountbatten, Supreme Allied Commander, South-East Asia. This dramatic picture shows the smoke pall over Fort Dufferin after bombing.

GREAT ADVANCES WEST OF RHINE. By 20 March all German resistance west of the Rhine had collapsed, and on that day the American Third Army advanced more than twenty miles to capture the ancient city of Worms. Troops under General Patch also overran the rich industrial area of the Saar Basin with its capital, Saarbrucken, while on 21 March the Seventh Army entered Ludwigshafen, a centre of the German chemical industry. Tens of

thousands of prisoners surrendered to the Allies on this front, where over 5,000 square miles of Reich territory had been taken by the Third Army alone. The pictures at the top of these pages show homeless inhabitants of Saarbrucken leaving with their belongings after the city had been taken over by the American forces; bottom left, U.S. troops marching in one of the city's main streets; bottom right, searching for the last hidden snipers.

GERMAN SUPPLY TOWNS BOMBED

On 22 March Anglo-American bombing of the enemy's Rhine defences reached its climax when in a dawn to dusk assault over 7,300 sorties were flown. The scale of these air operations was as great as in the peak stages of the Normandy campaign, and the wholly devastating offensive in which many thousands of bombers and fighter bombers took part proved a decisive factor in the immediate success of the military operations which followed. Great loads of high-explosive and incendiary bombs went down on important targets in the road-rail network leading east from the Rhine to the North German plain. Enemy troop concentrations, advanced defence bases (all packed with troops and supplies), and Rhine crossings still in enemy hands, were also attacked. By night-fall mile after mile of German front-line towns and villages were blazing, many of them reduced to smoking ruins, and all traffic behind the enemy's front on the Lower Rhine had been brought practically to a standstill. Great columns of refugees were seen by Allied airmen crowding the roads north of the Lower Rhine, fleeing towards Munster, Osnabruck and the North German plain. Allied aircraft met practically no opposition from the Luftwaffe, for from all operations during the day and previous night only six machines were lost. Picture shows vast smoke clouds rising from many fires in Bocholt, a German advance base heavily attacked by aircraft of Bomber Command.

BATTLE OF THE RHINE

On 24 March, in the biggest military operations since D-Day, British, Canadian and American troops of Twenty-first Army Group crossed the Rhine in strength. This assault against the last great natural barrier in the west was under the overall command of Field-Marshal Montgomery. Under cover of the greatest smoke-screen ever laid down, Montgomery's forces poured over the Rhine at Wesel, and by nightfall that town was taken and bridgeheads had been established. Simultaneously, the biggest airborne operation of the war was carried out by the British 6th and American 17th Airborne Divisions. Of the 8,000 prisoners captured in the first day by Twenty-first Army Group, more than one-third were taken by airborne troops. By 27 March Montgomery's men were about 280 miles from Berlin, while farther south Patton's forces were only 240 miles from Marshal Koniev's troops in Czechoslovakia. On the right, British troops are seen crossing the Rhine at dawn; bottom left, R.E.s prepare to ferry the Rhine; bottom right, troops crossing river under cover of smoke screen.

BRIDGEHEADS ESTABLISHED. By 25 March the four separate bridgeheads across the Rhine in the Wesel-Rees area had been merged into a solid front some thirty miles wide, and strong reinforcements of men and armour were crossing the river. Everywhere the airborne troops had linked up with the infantry. Except in and around Rees, where enemy paratroopers showed fanatical resistance, German opposition was disorganized. Mr. Churchill is shown on left crossing the Rhine with Montgomery. Above, Allied supplies pour over the river.

DEAD GERMAN TOWN. This striking picture shows the shattered remains of Wesel, the vital German strong-
point and key defensive position on the east bank of the Rhine, after it had been taken by British Commando
troops only four hours after they had crossed the Rhine as the spearhead of Twenty-first Army Group. Badly

blitzed in a series of earlier air and artillery bombardments, which immediately preceded the Rhine crossings, the town was virtually reduced to little more than a vast heap of rubble in a final all-out attack by the Allied Air Forces during the night of 23-24 March. The air blows against Wesel completely obliterated its defences.

AIRBORNE ARMY OVER THE RHINE. In the mighty airborne operation over the Rhine more than 3,000 transport aircraft took part. These were flown from nearly thirty bases in Britain and on the Continent and were well protected by strong forces of fighters. They dropped parachutists and glider-borne troops in and behind the enemy's lines of defence east of the Rhine and ahead of the assault troops storming across the river. On the left-hand page some of the gliders are seen over Germany ; above, parachutes fill the sky as airborne men descend.

SUCCESS OF AIRBORNE ACTION. That the lessons of the gallant failure at Arnhem had been well learnt was shown in the conspicuous success that was achieved in the airborne crossing of the Rhine. The operation had been brilliantly timed and planned to the last detail and in spite of the considerable risks involved, everything went according to schedule. Within half an hour of landing the British airborne men had seized their main objectives, captured large numbers of prisoners, and gained control of six bridges over the Ijssel, beyond the Rhine. Equal successes attended the Americans, and losses were slight. Left, a paratrooper helps wounded comrade during the fighting for a vital objective; the photographs above show the airborne troops in action.

END OF GERMAN V-2 ATTACKS. The last rocket-bomb fell at Orpington, Kent, on 27 March, after attacks on Southern England had lasted over six months. In all, 1,050 rockets fell here, killing 2,754 persons and seriously injuring 6,523. The picture shows one of the last and worst incidents at Smithfield Market, London, where 110 people were killed and 123 seriously injured when pavements and market stalls were crowded with shoppers.

Wrecked German village

CANADIANS ADVANCE INTO GERMANY. On 30 March the frontier town of Emmerich, on the Dutch-German border, fell to Canadian troops of Twenty-first Army Group after very fierce fighting with German parachute regiments. Bocholt, with huge marshalling yards and textile factories, was also captured. The enemy was fighting desperately to keep open supply lines from Holland. Above, Canadian tanks in a wrecked village of Germany.

GERMAN INDUSTRIAL CITIES FALL. By 29 March the Allies were driving deep into the heart of industrial Germany and cities which had built and nourished the Nazi war machine fell in rapid succession. Mannheim, which had some of the largest engineering plants in the Reich, surrendered to the U.S. Seventh Army on 29 March. Next day the Allies captured Frankfurt-on-Main, where hardly a house remained, and Duisburg, largest inland port in the world. Above, carrying water in devastated Mannheim; opposite, in captured Duisburg.

RED ARMY CAPTURES DANZIG. On 30 March a Soviet Order of the Day announced that troops of the Second White Russian front had captured Danzig, "an important port and first-class naval base on the Baltic." During the hard-fought battle for the city nearly 40,000 Germans were killed and over 10,000 taken prisoner. The vast booty

captured by the Russians included 140 tanks and self-propelled guns, 358 field guns, 84 aircraft, 306 railway locomotives, over 150 ships of various tonnages and 45 U-boats. Polish troops under General Poplavsky took a prominent part with the Russians in the city's capture. Above, Red Army mechanized units advancing on Danzig.

ALLIES CAPTURE MORE GERMAN TOWNS. The American Seventh Army made rapid progress following their breakthrough on the Middle Rhine and by 1 April they were in complete occupation of the ancient city of Heidelberg. This fell into American hands intact and virtually undamaged, its famous university, which is the oldest in Germany, being spared any destruction. Farther north, on the First Army front, there was very heavy street fighting for the industrial city of Kassel, the ruins of which were formally surrendered by the German commandant on

4 April. Kassel was a most important centre of German war production, and here was situated the great Henschel locomotive works, one of the largest in the Reich, which had also turned out quantities of Tiger and Panther tanks. This and other large factories had been wrecked by many Allied bombing raids in the previous months. Top left, snipers rounded up in Heidelberg; bottom left, Germans survey devastation in Bettenhausen, a suburb of Kassel; top right, civilians in a burning street; Allied infantrymen scouting for snipers in Zweibrucken.

WEHRMACHT IN DEFEAT. By 2 April troops under General Dempsey were racing across North-West Germany 100 miles from the Rhine. Farther south the Americans captured Paderborn and cut off the industrial Ruhr with some 100,000 German troops in the net. Everywhere the speed and weight of the Allied onslaught

had broken morale in the German army, and the enemy was surrendering at the rate of 10,000 or 12,000 a day. On one day alone over 40,000 prisoners were herded into cages. Allied progress was in fact held up by masses of prisoners on the roads and problems of dealing with them. Here is one concentration of 16,000 Germans.

GERMAN RAIL CENTRE CAPTURED. When Allied troops entered Hamm, in the northern Ruhr, on 3 April, they saw for themselves the highly satisfactory results of concentrated bombing. Nearly a hundred single raids were made on the famous railway marshalling yards during the war, and thousands of forced labourers, mainly from occupied countries, were employed on constant repair work. Some of the devastation in the Hamm yards is pictured on the opposite page. Above, the aftermath of heavy bombing attacks in a large Ruhr factory.

CANADIANS ADVANCE IN HOLLAND. After the Canadian First Army had crossed the German-Dutch frontier they made steady progress northwards across Holland towards the Zuider Zee, despite stiffening opposition from the large number of enemy troops there. On 7 April the ancient town of Zutphen on the Ijssel River, where Sir Philip Sidney died in 1586, was captured, together with many of the surrounding V-bomb bases. The pictures show : top left, wreckage in a main street of Zutphen and Dutch flags flying from houses in the background ; bottom left, launching ramp of a flying bomb site overrun near Zutphen ; above, searching for snipers in a village.

181

FINAL PUSH IN ITALY

On 9 April the Eighth Army launched a powerful assault against the enemy's defences on the Senio River. Flame-throwers played a big part in the initial attack which was preceded by a tremendous artillery barrage. By midday on 10 April over 1,200 prisoners had been taken and the advance was going well. Great support was given by the air forces which dropped some 350,000 fragmentation bombs on German troops and fortifications. It was reported that Italian forces were taking part in the offensive. Fierce fighting continued for several days, though excellent progress was made by both Eighth and Fifth Armies in the face of strong opposition. By 22 April the enemy was fast retreating to the Po River. Right, Allied flame-throwers in action; below, the infantry following up; opposite page, an Allied convoy of jeeps moving up through a ruined village.

ITALIAN OFFENSIVE GOES WELL
Indian troops of the Eighth Army advance over a mountain ridge near Bologna

HANOVER FALLS TO AMERICANS. Continuing their swift advance north-east from Hamm, the U.S. Ninth Army occupied the two great cities of Hanover and Essen on 10 April. In Hanover, contrary to the practice in nearly all German towns and villages overrun by the Allies, not a single white flag was shown, following a warning by the local Gauleiter that any one doing so would be shot immediately. Nevertheless, thousands of citizens lined the streets to watch the battle raging through the city. Top left, German civilians looting in Hanover soon after it fell to Allied troops; bottom left, wrecked rail-yards at Hanover; above, German prisoners being marched away.

PRESIDENT ROOSEVELT DIES. A deeply shocked world received the news of the sudden passing of Franklin D. Roosevelt on 12 April. He died peacefully at his country home at Warm Springs, Georgia, after an attack of cerebral hæmorrhage brought on by the strain of his heavy duties. At the age of sixty-three, Roosevelt had achieved the unprecedented record of being elected for four consecutive terms of office as President of

the United States of America, and had guided that nation with supreme courage, foresight and wisdom through the most difficult period of its history. He crossed the Atlantic several times to attend famous conferences with Mr. Churchill and Marshal Stalin. The new President was Senator Harry S. Truman, who had held the office of Vice-President since January, 1945. Picture shows the late President's funeral procession in Washington.

RUSSIANS CAPTURE VIENNA

After several days of hard fighting and violent street battles Vienna, capital of Austria, was liberated by Red Army troops under Marshal Tolbukhin on 13 April. Although the battle for the city had begun in mid-March after the great Russian victory at Lake Balaton, fighting in the streets of the capital lasted less than one week and thus most of its famous and beautiful buildings were spared. The Red Army took more than 130,000 prisoners during the battles on the approaches to Vienna and routed no fewer than eleven German tank divisions. Austrian anti-fascists helped the Russians in final mopping-up operations. Left, Soviet motorized troops fighting in Vienna; bottom left, Red infantrymen march through city; bottom right, civilians help to clear wreckage of demolished city buildings.

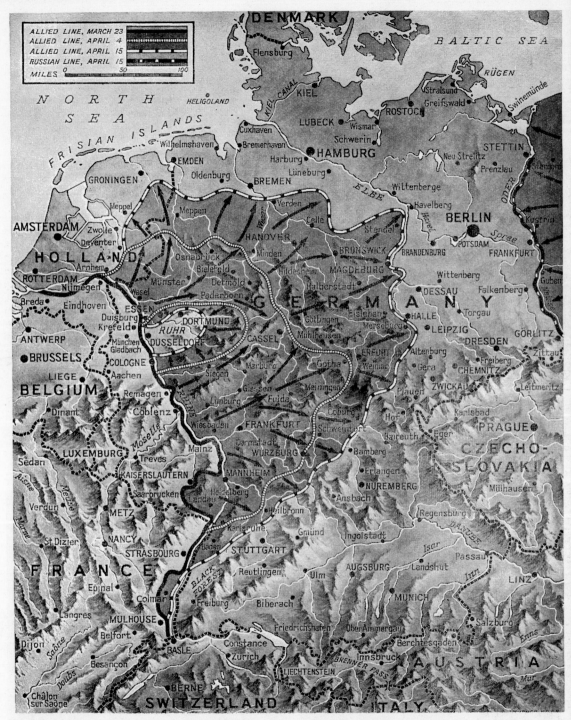

BEYOND THE RHINE. Following the crossings of the Rhine in March, Anglo-American mechanized columns fanned out widely across north-west and central Germany, meeting very little opposition from the rapidly crumbling Wehrmacht. One great city after another fell to the victorious Allies, while some 100,000 enemy troops were sealed off in the Ruhr pocket. The map above shows the sweeping movement towards the centre of the Reich and the Czechoslovak border, and the British advance in the north to cut off Holland. It also shows positions reached by the Western Allies and the Red Army on 15 April. Right, British armoured cars advance to the River Elbe.

NAZI CRUELTY EXPOSED TO THE WORLD. As the Allies advanced deeper into the Reich they overran some of the worst of the infamous Nazi concentration camps at Dachau, Belsen, Buchenwald, Nordhausen, Ohrdruf and elsewhere. All these camps revealed horrors and bestial cruelty on a scale that far exceeded those found

in the former Nazi-occupied countries. In each one thousands of men, women and children, chiefly Jewish, and from almost every part of Europe, had been systematically starved, tortured and murdered by brutal S.S. guards. The picture on these pages shows a communal grave into which the dead and dying were thrown by the Nazis.

HORRORS OF BELSEN CAMP

The indescribable scenes of horror, mass cruelty and degradation revealed in the huge concentration camp at Belsen shocked the civilized world. When the camp was overrun by the British Second Army more than 60,000 civilians, mostly suffering from typhus and other dreaded diseases, were herded together there. Hundreds were dying every day in the appallingly overcrowded huts, and many of the living, mere skeletons of skin and bone, were too weak to be removed. Many of the inmates had been disfigured for life by continuous beatings and prolonged suffering. Left, Josef Kramer (the "Beast of Belsen"), the camp commander under British guard; below, German women view atrocities; opposite page, bodies of children starved to death at Belsen.

FALL OF LEIPZIG

On 19 April the American First Army captured Leipzig, fifth largest city of Germany and capital of Saxony. Around the railway station and on the city outskirts fanatical S.S. troops resisted up to the last until they were forced into surrender by heavy artillery fire at point-blank range. Thousands of British, American and Russian prisoners of war were liberated from camps in the immediate neighbourhood. After the German garrison at Leipzig had finally surrendered, looting by civilians broke out in the city and the picture, left, shows a raid on a train in the station. Above, U.S. troops entering a blazing suburb of the city.

ALLIES CAPTURE MUNICH. In the last days of April the American Seventh Army under General Patch cleared large areas of Southern Germany and their armoured columns drove on into the passes of the Austrian Alps. Most important of the towns captured was Munich, capital of Bavaria, and cradle of the Nazi movement. Most of the enemy garrison had withdrawn when the Americans arrived, leaving only snipers to be dealt with. Top, U.S. troops pass the famous beer cellar where Hitler held the first Nazi meetings; below, Americans occupy city.

SURRENDER OF NUREMBERG

On the evening of 20 April, as hundreds of American tanks rolled into the bomb-shattered city, all enemy resistance ceased in Nuremberg. The surrender of this great city, one of the oldest in Germany, was a bitter blow to the Nazis inasmuch as it had been their chief shrine ever since they came to power. All the great party rallies had been held in the vast stadium which had been specially built for the purpose, while the city's chief square was appropriately named the Adolf Hitler Platz. That square, like many other parts of Nuremberg, had suffered much destruction not only from Allied bombing, but from heavy artillery shelling made necessary by the last dogged resistance put up by picked S.S. defenders. During the war Nuremberg had been a busy centre of production for the German war machine having many large engineering and electrical industries which turned out tanks, motor vehicles, aircraft parts, electrical equipment and so on. Most of these factories had been destroyed or badly damaged by the effective day and night attacks carried out by the Anglo-American air forces during the preceding months. On 21 April about 14,000 prisoners of war, of whom nearly 1,000 were British, were liberated in the Nuremberg area. American tanks are seen here progressing at slow pace among the rubble heaps that were once the streets of Nuremberg.

WESTERN ALLIES LINK UP WITH RUSSIANS. On the afternoon of 25 April the first contact between the Americans and Russians was made at Torgau, on the River Elbe, about 100 miles from Berlin. To mark this historic meeting between the American First Army and the 58th Guards Division of the Red Army three simultaneous announcements were made from London, Washington and Moscow, and in the Russian capital a salute from 324 guns was fired. Above, U.S. and Russian units meet; left, a Soviet officer greeting Field-Marshal Montgomery.

SAN FRANCISCO CONFERENCE

On 25 April an historic conference, attended by representatives from all the United Nations, opened in the Opera House at San Francisco, California. The object of this great meeting was to lay the foundations of a new World Security Organization to ensure the future peace of mankind. The chief delegates of the leading powers at the conference were Mr. Anthony Eden, Mr. Attlee and Lord Halifax (Great Britain); Mr. Stettinius and Mr. Cordell Hull (U.S.A.); M. Molotov (Soviet Union); Dr. T. V. Soong and Dr. Wellington Koo (China); and M. Georges Bidault (France). After Mr. Stettinius had welcomed the delegates from forty-six nations to San Francisco on behalf of the United States, the conference was ceremonially opened with a broadcast speech from Washington by President Truman who declared that this was the most important conference in history. Exactly two months later the peace charter was signed and the picture, left, shows the delegates applauding the announcement by Lord Halifax. Bottom left, Mr. Eden, Mr. Stettinius, M. Molotov and Dr. Soong; below, President Truman addressing the final session of the conference.

GREAT GERMAN PORT CAPTURED. After two days and nights of fierce street fighting the great port of
Bremen was captured by British troops on 26 April. Much of the city was laid in ruins through the German
commander's decision to hold Bremen to the last, for his failure to surrender quickly brought the full weight of

the Allied bombing forces, together with intensive artillery shelling into the attack. Scottish troops of the 52nd (Lowland) Division with battalions of the Manchester Regiment, burned their way through enemy strong-points in the city before it fell. Here is a scene at the British victory parade in Bremerhaven, outer suburb of Bremen.

HEAVY FIGHTING IN OKINAWA CAMPAIGN. Throughout April there was heavy and continuous fighting on the small Pacific island of Okinawa, an important air base only 325 miles from the mainland of Japan. The American landing on the island earlier in the month was the largest of the Pacific War to date. The conquest of this vital strip of land was no easy task for the men of the U.S. Tenth Army. Above, an American flame-throwing tank lays a barrage of fire on a hillside; top right, flame-throwers in action; below, tanks and infantry advancing.

End of a Dictator

MUSSOLINI PAYS THE PENALTY. On 28 April Mussolini, together with his mistress, Clara Petacci, was captured by a group of Italian partisans in a village beside Lake Como, in Northern Italy. Only a few hours after his arrest the former arrogant dictator was tried, sentenced to death, and shot by his captors. Twelve members of his Fascist cabinet were shot at the same time. Soon after the sentence had been carried out the bodies of Mussolini and Clara Petacci were taken to Milan where they were hung upside down in one of the city's squares.

Germans surrender in Italy

FIGHTING ENDS IN ITALY

The unconditional surrender of nearly one million German troops fighting in Italy was signed at Caserta on 29 April after the Eighth and Fifth Armies had completed their swift advance across the North Italian plain. The instrument of surrender was signed by two German plenipotentiaries in civilian attire and Lieutenant-General W. D. Morgan, Chief of Staff at Allied Force Headquarters. In a message to his victorious troops on 2 May Field-Marshal Alexander declared: "After nearly two years of hard and continuous fighting you stand today as victors in the Italian campaign. You may well be proud of this great campaign which will long live in history as one of the greatest and most successful ever waged." Above, the surrender ceremony; left, Field-Marshal Alexander greets General Mark Clark in North Italy.

RED ARMY IN BERLIN

On 2 May Berlin was occupied by Russian troops under Marshals Zhukov and Koniev after seventeen days of fierce fighting. In the afternoon the city's garrison, with General Weilding and his staff at their head, laid down their arms and by evening over 70,000 prisoners had been taken in the German capital. The battle for Berlin, which Hitler once boasted would never capitulate, was extremely bitter with house-to-house fighting in every street. For several days before the end came many parts of the city were ablaze. Every cellar and air raid shelter was converted into a strong-point, and there was fighting even in the tunnels of the underground railway and the sewers. Most of the city was in ruins. Right, Russian tanks advancing in Berlin; bottom left, aftermath of a street battle; bottom right, German troops leaving the ruined capital as prisoners.

END OF BURMA CAMPAIGN. On 3 May British and Indian troops liberated the great port of Rangoon, capital of Burma, just over three years since it fell to the Japanese in March, 1942. The recapture of this city, which virtually ended the long and difficult campaign in Burma, trapped all the Japanese troops to the west of the Irrawaddy, while those to the east of the river were left to fight their way into Siam over wild jungle country. The speed of landing operations at Rangoon brought about the city's liberation just ten days before the monsoon broke, and so hastened the disintegration of the remaining Japanese forces in the country. During the Burma campaign British, Indian and African troops covered over 1,000 miles of the worst country in the world, under the worst climate and conditions, killing 97,000 Japanese and wounding 250,000 of the enemy. Above, a 25-pounder gun is taken ashore at Rangoon; top left, British mopping-up in Pegu; bottom left, Jap prisoner led away.

GERMANS SIGN UNCONDITIONAL SURRENDER. On 4 May Field-Marshal Montgomery received a dele-gation of German officers who agreed to the unconditional surrender of the German forces in North-West Germany, Holland and Denmark. Early on 7 May the terms were signed at General Eisenhower's headquarters at Rheims. General Jodl signed on behalf of the German High Command, while Generals Bedell Smith, Francois Sevez and Susloparov signed for the Allies. On 9 May terms of unconditional surrender were also signed in Berlin, where Field-Marshal Keitel was the chief German delegate and the Allied representatives were led by Air Chief Marshal Tedder, General Spaatz, General de Lattre de Tassigny and Marshal Zhukov. Pictures taken at these historic meetings show: above, German delegates at Field-Marshal Montgomery's headquarters; top right, ceremony at Rheims; below, Field-Marshal Wilhelm Keitel signs the ratified terms of unconditional surrender in Berlin.

ALLIED LINES SEPT. 3, 1944
ALLIED LINES APRIL 15, 1945
ALLIED LINES APRIL 26, 1945
MILES 0   100   200   300

NORWAY

OSLO

SWEDE

GERMAN FORCES
SURRENDERED, MAY 8

STOCKHO

GÖTEBORG

NORTH
SEA

DENMARK
GERMAN FORCES
SURRENDERED, MAY 4

COPENHAGEN

Esbjerg

BALT

Kiel   Rostock
HAMBURG   Kolberg
SURRENDERED, MAY 3   Belgar

Emden   Bremen   Stettin

Groningen   Elbe
AMSTERDAM   BERLIN
ROTTERDAM   HOLLAND   Munster   Hanover   SURRENDERED, MAY 2
LONDON   Magdeburg   Frankfurt   Poz
Ostend   Oder
Dunkirk   G E R M A N Y
Calais   RUHR   BRESLA
Boulogne   ANTWERP   COLOGNE   Cassel   LEIPZIG
Lille   BRUSSELS   Bonn   Erfurt   DRESDEN
ENGLISH CHANNEL   BELGIUM   Coblenz   PRAGUE
Cherbourg   LUXEMBURG   FRANKFURT   PILSEN   CZECH
Havre   Amiens   SAAR   Mannheim   Nüremberg
Caen   Rouen   Metz   Karlsruhe
Argentan   Reims   Nancy   Stuttgart   Augsburg   LINZ   VIENNA
Rennes   PARIS   Marne   STRASBOURG   Danube   Salzburg
Le Mans   Orleans   Troyes   Mulhouse   Freiburg   MUNICH   Berchtesgaden
St.Nazaire   Nevers   Dijon   Basle   Innsbruck   AUSTRIA
Nantes   Tours   F R A N C E   BERNE   Klagenfurt   Graz
Poitiers   SWITZERLAND   Udine   Ljubljana
La Rochelle   Vichy   MILAN   GERMAN FORCES   TRIESTE
Limoges   Clermont   LYONS   Padua   SURRENDERED, MAY 2
BORDEAUX   Ferrand   St.Etienne   VENICE   Fiume
Garonne   Valence   TURIN   Modena
Bayonne   Montauban   Avignon   GENOA   Bologna   Ravenna   ADRIATIC
TOULOUSE   Spezia   Rimini   Zara   Sp
Montpellier   NICE   Pisa   FLORENCE   Ancona
MARSEILLES   Leghorn   Perugia
S P A I N   Toulon   CORSICA   I T A L Y   Pescara
MEDITERRANEAN   SEA   ROME

S.J.TURNER, F.R.G.S.

TOTAL DEFEAT OF GERMANY

MAY, 1945

The tremendous achievements of Allied arms in the last eight months of the war against Nazi Germany can be appreciated from this map of all the fronts in Europe, specially drawn by S. J. Turner, F.R.G.S. In September, 1944, when the sixth year of the war opened, the Western Allies were still fighting in France and Belgium, although at many points they had the enemy on the run. Nevertheless, the frontiers of the Reich itself had yet to be penetrated and the liberation of Holland was still many months away. In the East, the Red Army had finally driven the enemy from all Soviet territory, but nearly 400 miles still lay between them and Berlin. In Italy, the Fifth and Eighth Armies were beginning their successful attack against the German-held Gothic Line in the Northern Apennines. The winter months of 1944-1945 saw hard fighting on all fronts. In the West there was the large-scale German counter-attack in the Ardennes, south of Liége, while in the East there was determined enemy resistance to be overcome in East Prussia, around Budapest and elsewhere. By the spring, however, the hard crust of the German outer defences had been broken and the total defeat of Hitler's armies had become a certainty. Once the powerful Anglo-American armies had crossed the Rhine, they swept into the heart of the Reich, occupying the great towns and cities of Western Germany with hardly a struggle. Meanwhile, the Russians crushed all resistance in East Prussia, smashed their way into Berlin, and drove up the Danube valley to Vienna. The first German armies to lay down their arms were those in Italy, where surrender was completed on 2 May; last to surrender were the German forces in Norway (about 400,000 men) on 8 May. After that date only a few scattered bands of Nazis remained to be rounded up. These, together with fugitive German leaders and war criminals, were found chiefly in the mountainous regions of Austria.

VICTORY IN EUROPE

On 8 May the Prime Minister, Mr. Winston Churchill, broadcast a victory message to millions of listeners in Great Britain and throughout the British Commonwealth. He said: "Yesterday morning at 2.41 a.m. at Headquarters, General Jodl, the representative of the German High Command, and of Grand Admiral Donitz, the designated head of the German State, signed the pact of unconditional surrender of all German land, sea and air forces in Europe to the Allied Expeditionary Force, and simultaneously to the Russian High Command. General Beddell Smith, Chief of Staff of the Allied Expeditionary Force, and General Francois Sevez signed the document on behalf of the Supreme Commander of the Allied Expeditionary Force, and General Susloparov signed on behalf of the Russian High Command. Today this agreement will be ratified in Berlin, where Air Chief Marshal Tedder, Deputy Supreme Commander of the Allied Expeditionary Force, and General de Lattre de Tassigny will sign on behalf of General Eisenhower. Marshal Zhukov will sign on behalf of the Soviet High Command. The German representative will be Field-Marshal Keitel, Chief of the High Command, and the Commanders-in-Chief of the German Army, Navy and Air Forces. Hostilities will end officially at one minute after midnight tonight (Tuesday), but in the interest of saving lives the 'Cease Fire' began yesterday to be sounded all along the front, and our dear Channel Islands are also to be freed today. . . . Today, perhaps, we shall think mostly of ourselves. Tomorrow we shall pay a particular tribute to our Russian comrades whose prowess in the field has been one of the grand contributions to the general victory. The German war is therefore at an end. After years of preparation, Germany hurled herself upon Poland . . . and in pursuance of our guarantee to Poland, and in agreement with the French Republic, Great Britain, the British Empire and Commonwealth of Nations, declared war upon this foul aggression. After gallant France had been struck down, we, from this island and our united Empire, maintained the struggle single-handed for a whole year until we were joined by the military might of Soviet Russia and later by the overwhelming power and resources of the United States of America. Finally, almost the whole world was combined against the evil-doers who are now prostrate before us. Our gratitude to our splendid allies goes forth from all our hearts in this island and throughout the British Empire. We may allow ourselves a brief period of rejoicing, but let us not forget for a moment the toil and efforts that lie ahead. Japan, with all her treachery and greed, remains unsubdued. The injury she has inflicted on Great Britain, the United States, and other countries, and her detestable cruelties call for justice and retribution. We must now devote all our strength and resources to the completion of our task, both at home and abroad. Advance, Britannia! Long live the cause of freedom!
God save the King!"

VE-DAY CELEBRATIONS IN LONDON. Soon after the Prime Minister had broadcast the official declaration of peace in Europe, there were remarkable scenes in the towns and cities all over Great Britain and in Northern Ireland. Everywhere the people demonstrated their glad feelings that the fighting on the Continent was at last over and that air raids and blackouts were things of the past. The biggest and most enthusiastic crowds of all were witnessed in London, and these began to gather in the main streets and squares some hours before Mr. Churchill made his broadcast speech. The two main centres to which the vast crowds flocked on VE-Day were Buckingham Palace and Parliament Square, at the foot of Whitehall. By early afternoon the dense masses of people assembled in the square around the Victoria Memorial facing the forecourt of the Palace numbered several thousands, and thousands more had arrived there before dusk. Soon after three o'clock the King and Queen made their first appearance on the balcony, where, with Princess Elizabeth and Princess Margaret Rose, they received tumultuous cheers from the crowds below. Later in the afternoon the Royal Family was joined on the balcony by the Prime Minister, and the roar of welcome was kept up for more than five minutes. In Parliament

Square and Whitehall the crowds stretched right across the roadways and they gave a tremendous ovation to Mr. Churchill when he appeared with other members of the War Cabinet on the balcony of the Ministry of Health. Speaking to the great crowd from the balcony the Prime Minister said: "This is your victory. It is the victory of the cause of freedom in every land. In all our long history we have never seen a greater day than this." Some of the interesting VE-Day scenes in London are pictured on these pages; top left, the King and Queen and the two Princesses, with the Prime Minister, acknowledge the loyal demonstration of the crowds in front of Buckingham Palace; bottom left, Mr. Churchill and Members of Parliament leave the House of Commons for Service of Thanksgiving at St. Margaret's, Westminster; top right, members of the War Cabinet on the Ministry of Health balcony (l. to r.), Mr. Oliver Lyttelton, Mr. Ernest Bevin, Mr. Churchill, Sir John Anderson, Lord Woolton and Mr. Herbert Morrison; bottom right, King George with his Ministers and Service Chiefs, front row (l. to r.), Mr. Churchill, King George, Mr. Bevin, Sir John Anderson; (centre row) Sir A. Sinclair, Lord Woolton, Mr. Lyttelton, Mr. Morrison, Sir Alan Brooke; (back row) Sir Edward Bridges, General Ismay, Sir Charles Portal, Sir A. Cunningham

REJOICING AND THANKSGIVING. On 9 May, which was also a public holiday throughout Great Britain, the lively scenes of the previous day were repeated. Again, London's Piccadilly Circus seemed to be the centre of the revels by night as well as day. Every city, however, had its bonfires and fireworks after dark and public buildings were floodlit. Top left, girls and soldiers in Piccadilly Circus; bottom left, tightly packed crowds before floodlit Buckingham Palace; above, Royal Procession leaves St. Paul's Cathedral after Thanksgiving Service.

VE-DAY IN PARIS AND NEW YORK. The news of Germany's defeat was acclaimed by millions of people throughout the world. In Paris, where sirens and artillery salvos heralded Europe's return to peace, vast crowds congregated in the city's squares and boulevards and around the Arc de Triomphe (pictures on opposite page). On the other side of the Atlantic New Yorkers went wild with joy, and there were public rejoicings and thanksgiving services in towns and cities all over the United States of America. Above, VE-Day in Wall Street, New York.

Jubilant crowds in Belgium.

PEACE RETURNS TO EUROPE

In the various countries of Europe which had suffered years of German occupation and terror, the day of final victory brought a feeling of relief as well as gladness. In Belgium, Holland, Denmark and Norway, civilians old and young thronged the streets of the great cities, the towns and villages to give expression to their feelings now that their regained freedom was firmly established. Everywhere there were special greetings for the British and American soldiers, sailors and airmen who had played so great a part in the liberation of Europe. Top left, crowds gather around U.S. vehicles in Brussels; bottom left, people running down a street in Rotterdam to meet Canadian food lorries on VE-Day; above, celebrations in Denmark; left, Norwegian nurses greet British paratroopers after their arrival in Oslo.

RUSSIA CELEBRATES PEACE. Throughout the Soviet Union victory over Germany was celebrated on 9 May after an early morning broadcast by Marshal Stalin. In Moscow tens of thousands of people gathered to sing and dance in Red Square and other public places, while victory demonstrations were staged outside the Allied embassies. Top, a British soldier being tossed by the crowds in Moscow; below, Red Army parade in Leningrad.

Czechoslovakia freed

LIBERATION OF PRAGUE. On 10 May, Prague, last capital of Allied Europe to be liberated, was entered by Russian tanks. The long-suffering citizens lined the streets and threw flowers at the soldiers as they passed. Some American troops who entered the city from the west also received a warm welcome. Top, Czechoslovak girls in national costume cheer their liberators; below, Dr. Benes, President of Czechoslovakia, welcomed back to Prague.

GERMAN U-BOATS SURRENDER

The first German submarine to surrender to the Royal Navy, U.249, was brought into Portland Harbour, in Weymouth Bay, on 10 May after having been escorted up the English Channel by British naval units. This submarine, which had surfaced some fifty miles off the coast of Cornwall, had five German officers and forty-three naval ratings on board. During the rest of the month aircraft of Coastal Command carried out the greatest anti-submarine patrol of the war in order to round up some seventy U-boats which were known to be roaming the seas at the time of the German surrender. Both the Royal Navy and the U.S. Navy joined in the search, and several U-boats were caught in distant parts of the Atlantic. Right, a U-boat lying off Westminster Pier, London; bottom left, German submarine surrenders to the U.S. Navy; bottom right, crew of the captured U.249 board a British ship at Portland Harbour.

NAZI WAR LEADERS ROUNDED UP. The death of Adolf Hitler was announced on the German radio by Grand Admiral Donitz, his successor, on 1 May. The body of Goebbels, who had poisoned himself, was found by the Russians in a Berlin air raid shelter. Other Nazi leaders and war criminals soon fell into Allied hands. Von Rundstedt, with his son, (top left) was captured at a Bavarian retreat by the Seventh Army. Goering (top

right), ex-Luftwaffe chief, surrendered at his hide-out near Salzburg on 10 May, the same day as von Kesselring (bottom right), former German C.-in-C. in Italy, gave himself up at Berchtesgaden. Himmler was captured near Hamburg on 21 May, but committed suicide by swallowing a phial of poison at British Army headquarters. Picture at bottom left shows Himmler dead. Centre, Albert Speer and Admiral Donitz with General Jodl.

TRAITORS IN CAPTIVITY. On 29 May William Joyce, known to the British public as "Lord Haw-Haw," was captured by troops of the Second Army on the Danish-German frontier near Flensburg. When questioned he made a movement with his right hand as if to draw a gun, and was promptly shot in the thigh. Joyce was then taken to Luneburg where the bullet was extracted, and about a fortnight later was flown to England to stand trial. Throughout the war Joyce broadcast Nazi propaganda to Britain from Germany. He is seen above on an army stretcher soon after he was captured. During the same month the Norwegian traitor, Vidkun Quisling, was brought to justice at Oslo (he is seen in court on the opposite page). He was the first major traitor of the war.

JAP SUICIDE BOMBERS HIT U.S. CARRIER. During the last months of the Far East war, Japanese suicide aircraft continued their desperate attacks on Allied shipping in a final bid to upset General MacArthur's invasion plans. Pictured here is the blazing aircraft carrier "Bunker Hill" (27,000 tons) after she had been hit with 550-lb. bombs by three enemy dive bombers. The aircraft crashed on to the carrier's decks, turning them into a blazing inferno and killing 392 officers and men. Eventually the fires were put out and the ship crossed the Pacific.

LANDINGS ON BORNEO

On 10 June troops of the Australian 9th Division went ashore in British North Borneo with very strong naval and air support. The landings were made without the loss of a man and against only scattered resistance. The important town and oil centre of Brunei was captured three days later and the Australians advanced rapidly along the coast towards the big Miri oilfields in Sarawak. A week later Australian forces made unopposed landings in Sarawak and took control of important oil regions which had been used by the Japs for over three years. Left, Japanese prisoners; above, Australians go ashore at Balikpapan. Smoke is seen pouring from the burning oil wells.

239

BRITISH TROOPS
IN BERLIN

On 4 July the British 7th Armoured Division (the famous "Desert Rats") with battalions of the Grenadier Guards and other regiments entered Berlin under command of Major-General L. O. Lyne to take over the occupation of the British zone. The Americans also occupied their own zone of the city following the inter-Allied decision that Greater Berlin should be garrisoned jointly by the Allies and not exclusively by the Russians, as hitherto. Later in the month Mr. Churchill visited Berlin and watched the great British victory parade staged in the city. Many regiments of the Army, as well as the Navy and R.A.F., took part in the proceedings, and the impressive parade of tanks along the Charlottenburger Chaussee is shown on these pages. Above, Grenadier Guards pass the saluting base where Mr. Churchill is seen taking the salute. Standing beside him on the platform are Field-Marshal Montgomery, Mr. Attlee, and Mr. Eden, together with military representatives from the United States, the Soviet Union and France.

PÉTAIN ON TRIAL. On 23 July the eighty-nine-year-old Marshal of France, Philippe Pétain, head of the former Vichy Government, appeared at the Palais de Justice in Paris on a charge of treason. During the three-week trial evidence for the prosecution was given by famous French political leaders, including two former premiers, M. Daladier and M. Reynaud. The traitor Pierre Laval appeared for the defence and is seen above giving evidence while Pétain listens. Pétain was sentenced to death, but the death penalty was commuted by General de Gaulle to imprisonment for life. Top right, Pétain in court; bottom right, listening to the evidence of M. Reynaud.

LABOUR WINS POWER IN BRITAIN

The result of Britain's general election, the first for ten years, was declared on 26 July, three weeks after polling day. For the first time in the history of the country the Socialist Party was returned to power with a large working majority, gaining nearly 400 seats in the House of Commons. Mr. Churchill, therefore, resigned the Premiership, and his place was taken by Mr. Attlee. Here is the new Labour Government photographed in the garden of No. 10 Downing Street, London. Back row (left to right): Mr. William Whiteley; Sir E. Bridges, Chief Whip; Sir F. Soskice, Solicitor-General; Mr. J. B. Hynd, Chancellor of the Duchy of Lancaster; the Earl of Listowel, Postmaster-General; Mr. E. J. Williams, Minister of Information; Mr. Lewis Silkin, Minister of Town and Country Planning; Mr. James Griffiths, Minister of National Insurance; Lord Winster, Minister of Civil Aviation; Mr. P. J. Noel-Baker, Minister of State; Mr. Wilfred Paling, Minister of Pensions; Sir Hartley Shawcross, Attorney-General; and Mr. Norman Brook. Centre row (left to right): Sir Ben Smith, Minister of Food; Mr. John Wilmot, Minister of Supply; Mr. Aneurin Bevan, Minister of Health; Mr. George Isaacs, Minister of Labour; Viscount Stansgate, Secretary of State for Air; Mr. G. Hall, Secretary for the Colonies; Lord Pethick-Lawrence, Secretary for India; Mr. J. Lawson, Secretary of State for War; Mr. J. Westwood, Secretary of State for Scotland; Mr. Emanuel Shinwell, Minister of Fuel and Power; Mr. T. Williams, Minister of Agriculture; Mr. G. Tomlinson, Minister of Works; Sir Alfred Barnes, Minister of Transport. Front row (left to right): Viscount Addison, Secretary for the Dominions; Lord Jowitt, Lord Chancellor; Sir Stafford Cripps, President of the Board of Trade; Mr. A. Greenwood, Lord Privy Seal; Mr. Ernest Bevin, Foreign Secretary; Mr. C. R. Attlee, Prime Minister; Mr. Herbert Morrison, Lord President of the Council; Mr. Hugh Dalton, Chancellor of the Exchequer; Mr. A. V. Alexander, First Lord of the Admiralty; Mr. Chuter Ede, Home Secretary; Miss Ellen Wilkinson, Education.

POTSDAM CONFERENCE. On 17 July the historic Three-Power Conference opened at the Cecilienhof Palace at Potsdam, outside Berlin, with Mr. Churchill, President Truman and Marshal Stalin heading the respective delegations. On 26 July a proclamation was issued to the Japanese people and signed by Mr. Churchill and President Truman, and approved by radio by Generalissimo Chiang Kai-shek. This offered Japan the choice of unconditional surrender or annihilation, and stated plainly the terms on which surrender would be accepted. As a result of the victory of the Labour Party in the British General Election, declared on 26 July, Mr. Churchill's place at Potsdam was taken by Mr. Attlee, the new Prime Minister, who had participated in the Conference from the beginning. Mr. Ernest Bevin, who succeeded Mr. Eden as Foreign Secretary, flew to Berlin with Mr. Attlee on 28 July. Early on 2 August the Potsdam Conference ended, and a long communique on the decisions taken there was issued simultaneously in London, Washington and Moscow. On the Allied attitude to Germany it was declared that "German militarism and Nazism will be extirpated and the Allies will take in agreement together, now and in the future, the other measures necessary to assure that Germany will never again threaten her neighbours or the peace of the world." Principles were established by the Three Powers governing the treatment of Germany during the initial period of Allied control, and the Potsdam declaration insisted on "the complete disarmament and demilitarization of Germany and the elimination or control of all German industry that could be used for military production." On the question of reparations: "that Germany be compelled to compensate to the greatest possible extent for the loss and suffering she has caused to the United Nations, and for which the German people cannot escape responsibility." It was also agreed at Potsdam that all the war criminals were to be brought to swift and sure justice. On the left the Conference is seen in session with Mr. Churchill, Mr. Eden, Mr. Attlee, President Truman and Marshal Stalin seated around the table. Above, Mr. Attlee, President Truman, Marshal Stalin with Admiral Leahy, Mr. Ernest Bevin, Mr. J. Byrnes and M. Molotov.

THE KING MEETS PRESIDENT TRUMAN. On his way home from the Potsdam Conference, President Truman broke his journey at Plymouth to exchange greetings with King George. This historic meeting took place on board the British battle-cruiser H.M.S. "Renown," anchored in Plymouth Sound about a mile from the American cruiser "Augusta" which was to take the President back to the United States. Just after midday the President left the "Augusta" to go aboard the "Renown" where, as pictured above, he was met at the head of the gangway by the King and entertained to luncheon. After lunch President Truman inspected a guard of honour of Royal Marines on board the battle-cruiser, and later King George paid a short visit to the President on board the "Augusta" before the cruiser left for America. As the U.S. ship passed the "Renown" the King stood at the salute.

ATOM BOMBS HIT JAPAN

In the late evening of 6 August the following dramatic announcement was made by President Truman: "Sixteen hours ago an American aeroplane dropped one bomb on Hiroshima, Japan. That bomb had more power than 20,000 tons of T.N.T., and more than 2,000 times the blast power of the British 'grand slam,' which is the largest bomb (22,000 lb.) yet used in the history of warfare." Thus the world heard of the first use of the atomic bomb, the result of the epoch-making discovery by the Allies of the splitting of the atom. Hiroshima, a great Japanese naval and army base with a population of about 340,000, was virtually disintegrated by the effect of the colossal explosion, and more than a third of its inhabitants were instantly killed or burned to death. The second atomic bomb was dropped on Nagasaki, another great city of Japan, on 9 August where the results were even more appalling. The vast cloud of smoke and flame following the explosion could be seen over 250 miles away. Above, the devastated city of Nagasaki after the atomic bomb raid. Rescue workers pick their way amid the rubble. Left, smoke, 20,000 ft. high, covers Hiroshima.

BRITAIN CELEBRATES FINAL VICTORY. On the morning of 14 August the Japanese Cabinet met and decided to accept the Allied surrender terms. At midnight the Prime Minister, Mr. Attlee, announced Japan's unconditional surrender and the end of the Second World War. An announcement was also made by President

Truman from the White House in Washington. The two following days were celebrated throughout Grea
Britain as a national holiday, and in every town and city there were remarkable scenes of care-free rejoicing.
On 15 August the King and Queen drove to Westminister in a carriage for the State opening of Parliament.

REJOICING IN THE HEART OF LONDON. Happy crowds thronged the streets and squares in the West End of London throughout the daylight hours of 15 August, but it was after dusk had fallen that the enthusiasm of the crowds reached its highest pitch. In such famous thoroughfares as Piccadilly Circus, where the picture

on these pages was taken after midnight, there was community singing and dancing on a grand scale around victory bonfires. After nearly six years of blackout and gloom, London was now transformed into a city of light. Apart from the glow of hundreds of bonfires and floodlighting, rockets and searchlight displays lit the sky.

JAPANESE SIGN FINAL SURRENDER. On Sunday, 2 September, Japan signed the document of final surrender, accepting the authority of General MacArthur, on board the American battleship "Missouri" anchored in Tokyo Bay. Eleven Japanese emissaries, including four diplomats in frock coats and top hats, were present at the ceremony, and the act of signing was carried out before General MacArthur, Supreme Allied Commander in the Far East. These radio pictures were taken aboard the "Missouri." Above, arrival of Shigemitsu, Jap Foreign Secretary; top left, General MacArthur (extreme left) watches Gen. Umaza sign; below, Admiral C. Nimitz signs.

FAITH CARRIED US TO VICTORY

"We kept faith with ourselves and with one another: we kept faith and unity with our great Allies. That faith, that unity, have carried us to victory through dangers which at times seemed overwhelming."

Extract from broadcast speech by
King George VI on 8th May, 1945

Made and printed in Great Britain by Odhams (Watford) Ltd., Watford.   Copyright S.258.11R.AF.